# 101 GREAT SCIENCE EXPERIMENTS

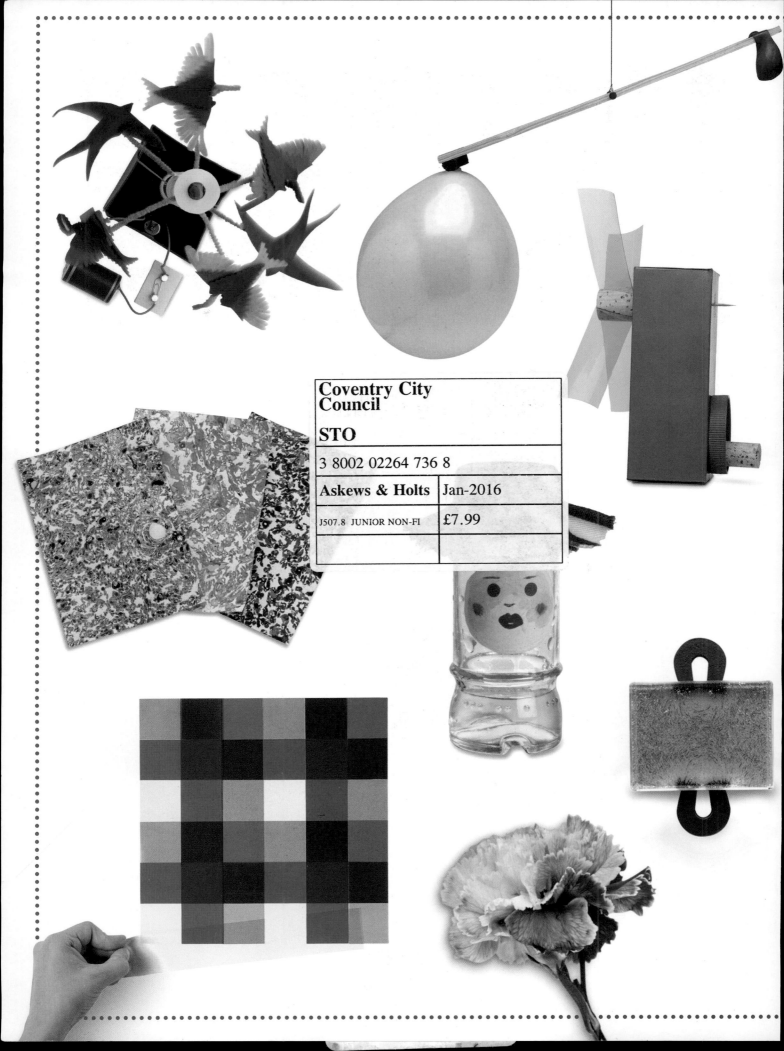

# 101 GREAT SCIENCE EXPERIMENTS

## Neil Ardley

LONDON, NEW YORK,
MELBOURNE, MUNICH, AND DELHI

**DK UK**

**Senior Editor:** Carron Brown
**Art Editor:** Mary Sandberg
**Creative Retouching:** Stefan Podhorodecki
**Managing Editor:** Linda Esposito
**Managing Art Editor:** Michael Duffy
**Category Publisher:** Andrew Macintyre
**Producer, Pre-production:** Lucy Sims
**Senior Producer:** Gemma Sharpe
**Jacket Editor:** Maud Whatley
**Jacket Designer:** Laura Brim
**Jacket Development Manager:** Sophia MTT
**Publishing Director:** Jonathan Metcalf
**Associate Publishing Director:** Liz Wheeler
**Art Director:** Phil Ormerod

**DK INDIA**

**Project Editor:** Bharti Bedi
**Project Art Editor:** Deep Shikha Walia
**Art Editors:** Dhirendra Singh, Shipra Jain
**Senior DTP Designer:** Harish Aggarwal
**DTP Designers:** Pawan Kumar,
Rajesh Singh Adhikari, Syed Farhad
**Managing Editor:** Alka Thakur Hazarika
**Managing Art Editor:** Romi Chakraborty
**CTS Manager:** Balwant Singh
**Production Manager:** Pankaj Sharma
**Jacket Designer:** Suhita Dharamjit
**Managing Jacket Editor:** Saloni Singh

First published in Great Britain in 1993
This edition first published in Great Britain in 2015 by
Dorling Kindersley Limited, 80 Strand, London WC2R ORL

Copyright © 1993, © 2015 Dorling Kindersley Limited
A Penguin Random House Company

4 6 8 10 9 7 5
274457 — Jan 2015

ISBN 978-0-2411-8513-1
Printed and bound in China

**BE A SAFE SCIENTIST**

**Always** follow all the steps in each experiment carefully.

**Take care**, especially when handling hot or heavy objects,
glass, scissors, knives, matches, candles, and batteries.

**Do not** smell things, put them in your ears or mouth,
or close to your eyes unless the book tells you to do so.

**Do not** play with electric switches, plugs, power points,
and electrical machines.

**Make sure** you clean up after each experiment.

This sign in a step means that **extra care** is needed.
You must ask an adult to help you with it.

# CONTENTS

## Air and Gases

## Water and Liquids

## Hot and Cold

## Light

# AIR AND GASES

Air is all around you – but you are hardly ever aware of it. You cannot see it, and you only feel it in a strong wind. But you breathe air all the time. It keeps you alive – and animals and plants too. Air is needed to burn fuel and to make many machines work. Aircraft use it when they fly. Air is made up of "gases" – substances which can change shape and "expand" or grow bigger to fill any shape or space.

## Air support

A bicycle pump forces more and more air into the inner tube of a tyre. The air pushes outwards on the walls of the tube. It pushes so hard that it can support the weight of both the bicycle and the rider.

## Buoyant balloons

These balloons contain a gas called helium. Helium is lighter than air, so it floats upwards, carrying the balloons with it.

*Nitrogen*

*Oxygen*

*Carbon dioxide and other gases*

*Argon*

## Big let down

As a parachute falls, air pushes upwards against it, so it drops slowly and safely to the ground. Air is made up of two main gases called nitrogen and oxygen, with small amounts of other gases.

## Big breath

When you breathe in, air enters your lungs. You can find out how much air your lungs can hold. Take a deep breath and then blow through a tube into an upturned jar of water. The air from your lungs pushes water out of the jar.

# ① Crush with air

Make a plastic bottle collapse without touching it! The air does the job for you. You cannot feel air, but it presses against every surface. This is called "air pressure".

**You will need:**

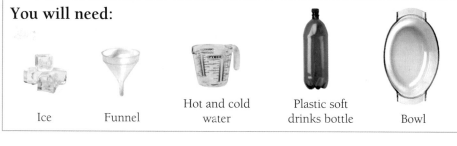

Ice     Funnel     Hot and cold water     Plastic soft drinks bottle     Bowl

**1.**  Stand the bottle upright in a bowl. Pour the hot water into it and leave it for a short time.

**2.** Screw the top on the bottle. Lay the bottle in the bowl and pour ice and cold water over it. Then stand it up.

**3.** As the warm air inside the bottle cools, it exerts less pressure. The pressure of the air outside is stronger and crushes the bottle.

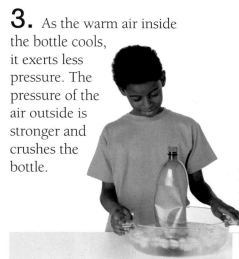

# ② Seal with air

Stop water falling out of an upturned glass. A card can stick to a glass and keep the water in it, as if by magic! Air pressure forces the card upwards, against the glass. The pressure is strong enough to stop the weight of the water pushing the card away.

**You will need:**

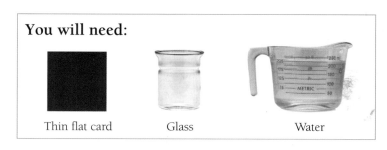

Thin flat card     Glass     Water

**1.** Hold the glass over a sink or a basin. Carefully pour some water into the glass.

*The rim must have no chips in it.*

**2.** Place the card on the glass. Hold it down so the card touches the rim all the way around.

**3.** Still holding the card, turn the glass upside-down. Let go of the card. The water stays in the glass!

# 3 Weigh some air

When something is very light, people often say "It's as light as air". But air is not light at all. Do this simple experiment to show that air is really quite heavy.

**1.** Use the ruler to find the centre of the wood. Then mark it.

**2.** 👫 Push a drawing pin into each side at the centre mark.

**3.** Tie the thread to the middle of the rubber band.

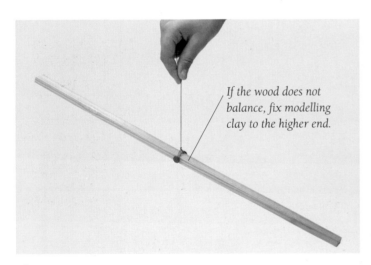

*If the wood does not balance, fix modelling clay to the higher end.*

**4.** Fix the loops of the rubber band around the drawing pins. Lift the wood by the thread. It should balance.

*Fix the neck of the balloon to the far end of the wood.*

**5.** Tape one of the balloons to one end of the wood.

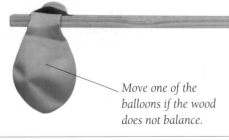

*Move one of the balloons if the wood does not balance.*

**6.** Tape the second balloon to the other end of the wood. Check that it still balances. Then remove one balloon and blow it up.

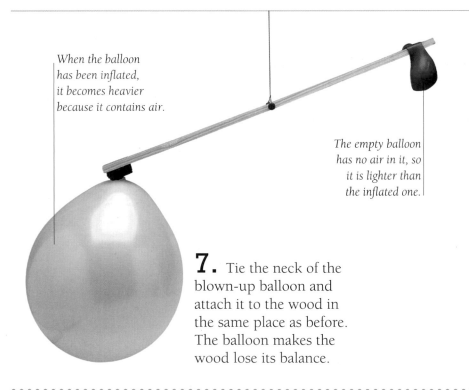

*When the balloon has been inflated, it becomes heavier because it contains air.*

*The empty balloon has no air in it, so it is lighter than the inflated one.*

**7.** Tie the neck of the blown-up balloon and attach it to the wood in the same place as before. The balloon makes the wood lose its balance.

**Drinking with a straw**
When you drink through a straw, the weight of the air helps you. The air above the drink pushes on the surface of the liquid. As you suck, it forces the liquid up through the straw to your mouth.

# 4 Discover the gases in the air

Put out a candle without blowing on it or touching it. When you do this experiment, you show that air is a mixture of invisible gases. One of these is especially important. It is oxygen, which is used when things burn and produce energy.

**You will need:**

Candle | Coloured water | Candle holder | Glass jar | Bowl

**1.** Put the candle in the holder and place it in the bowl. Then pour in the water.

**2.** 👤 Ask an adult to light the candle. Then place the jar over it. Leave it for a little while.

*The flame uses up the oxygen gas in the jar.*

*The water rises up to replace the oxygen. The remaining gas in the jar is mainly nitrogen.*

**Air and energy**
Like other cars, this racing car gets its energy from petrol burning in its engine. Burning fuel provides most of the energy we use for heating and powering machines. This process uses oxygen, which comes from the air around us.

**3.** At first, the water level in the jar rises, and then the flame suddenly goes out!

# 5 Form a gas

Inflate a balloon without blowing into it, or using a pump! You can do this by making a gas and then getting it to go into a balloon. The gas is called carbon dioxide. It is this gas that forms the bubbles in soda water and fizzy drinks.

**You will need:**

Vinegar

Sodium bicarbonate

Balloon

Funnel

Narrow-necked bottle

**1.** Pour some vinegar into the narrow-necked bottle until it is about a quarter full.

**2.** Using the funnel, fill the balloon with sodium bicarbonate powder.

**3.** Stretch the neck of the balloon over the neck of the bottle.

*Do not let the sodium bicarbonate escape from the balloon.*

**Exploding drink**
Shake a bottle of fizzy drink, then unscrew the cap. The drink fizzes up out of the bottle! Carbon dioxide gas is dissolved in the water in the drink. It is kept under pressure in the bottle. When you unscrew the cap, you reduce the pressure and the gas bubbles up out of the water.

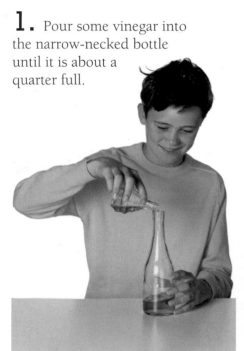

**4.** Lift the balloon so that the sodium bicarbonate falls into the bottle. The vinegar begins to fizz and the balloon slowly starts to inflate.

*As more gas forms, its pressure increases and the balloon expands.*

*The vinegar reacts with the sodium bicarbonate to release bubbles of carbon dioxide gas.*

# 6 Make a volcano erupt

Build a model volcano – then make it erupt! You can make "red-hot lava" flow down the sides. Although the lava is not real, your model volcano works like a real one.

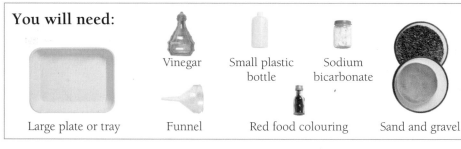

**You will need:**

Vinegar   Small plastic bottle   Sodium bicarbonate

Large plate or tray   Funnel   Red food colouring   Sand and gravel

**1.** Add red food colouring to the vinegar. This makes your "lava" red, like the real red-hot lava in a volcano.

**2.** Using the funnel, half fill the bottle with sodium bicarbonate. Then stand the bottle upright in the middle of the plate.

**3.** Pile gravel, then sand around the bottle to make the volcano. Quickly pour some red vinegar into the bottle and watch the volcano erupt!

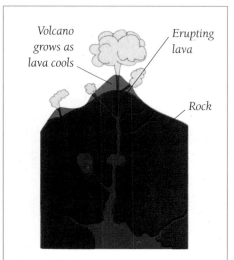

Volcano grows as lava cools

Erupting lava

Rock

**Exploding mountain**
A long pipe leads down from the top of a volcano to a deep underground chamber. There is melted rock in the chamber and very hot gases. The pressure of the gases sometimes forces the molten rock up the pipe to the surface. The red-hot melted rock, called "lava", erupts from the volcano and flows down its sides. There it cools and becomes solid. Eruptions cause the lava to build up and the volcano grows taller.

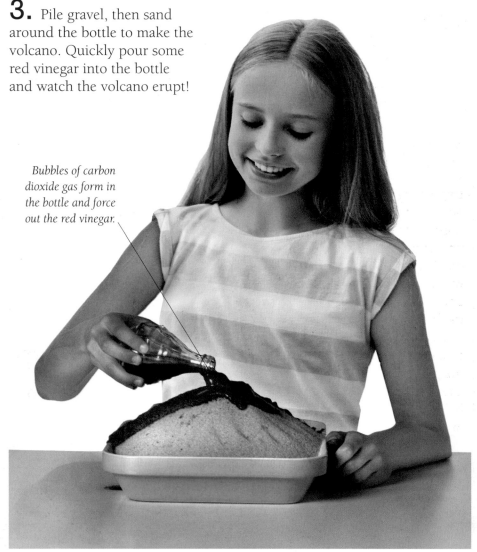

*Bubbles of carbon dioxide gas form in the bottle and force out the red vinegar.*

# 7 Make a wing fly

When birds and aircraft fly, moving air around their wings helps carry them high into the sky. Build and fly a model wing. It shows how moving air lifts up a wing and keeps it airborne.

**You will need:**

Short length of thread · Drinking straw · Hairdryer · Light, stiff paper

Sticky tape · Sharp pencil · Scissors

**1.** Fold the paper in two. Make one side of the fold a little smaller than the other.

**2.** Turn the paper over. Tape the edges together to make a wing shape.

**3.** Use the pencil to make two holes in the wing, one above the other.

**4.** 👫 Cut a piece of drinking straw, long enough to go through the holes.

**5.** Push the straw through the holes. Fix it firmly with sticky tape.

**6.** Feed the thread through the straw and tie it to something sturdy.

*Use the hairdryer to blow air over the curved top of the wing.*

**7.** 👫 Blow air on the wing. It rises up on the thread. It's amazing!

*As the air passes over the wing, it speeds up.*

*Still air under the wing has a higher pressure. It pushes the wing upwards.*

*As the air moves faster, its pressure falls.*

**Blow them apart?**
Tape cotton threads to two table-tennis balls and hang them about 15 cm (6 in) apart. Try blowing air between the balls. Instead of separating them, the moving air draws them together. As air moves, its pressure falls. The balls move towards the lower pressure, so they swing together.

# 8 Detect moisture in the air

Although air does not feel wet, it does contain moisture. Moisture in the air is called "humidity". The humidity of the air is constantly changing, as this experiment shows.

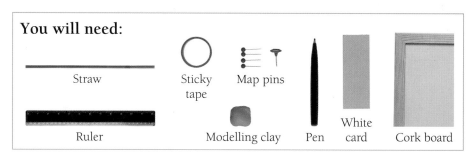

**You will need:**

Straw

Sticky tape

Map pins

Ruler

Modelling clay

Pen

White card

Cork board

**1.** With a ruler and pen, draw a scale on a piece of white card. Mark the scale at 2 mm (¹/₁₆ in) intervals. Pin the card to the cork board.

**2.** Push a pin through a straw near to one end. Pin the straw to the board, so that the long end points to the middle of the scale.

**3.** Press some modelling clay into the short end of the straw. Use just enough clay to balance the straw when the board is upright.

**4.** Get a friend to pull a hair carefully from your head – tell them not to pull too hard, or it will hurt!

*Hair absorbs and loses moisture easily.*

**5.** Tape one end of the hair to the short end of the straw and the other to the board's frame. Stand the board upright.

**Weather house**

This model house tells you what the weather is going to be like. The man comes out if the air is moist. This means that rain is likely. If the air is dry, the woman comes out. When she appears, it shows that there is dry weather ahead.

**6.** In dry air, the hair shrinks and pulls the straw up the scale. In moist air, the hair expands and the straw falls down the scale.

# ⑨ Measure the wind

You can feel the wind – but can you tell where it is coming from? It is important to know because a change in the wind can affect the weather. Make a wind vane to find the direction of the wind.

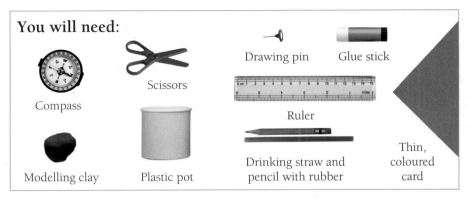

**You will need:**

Compass

Scissors

Drawing pin

Glue stick

Ruler

Modelling clay

Plastic pot

Drinking straw and pencil with rubber

Thin, coloured card

*Make sure the pot holds the pencil firmly.*

**1.** Use the pencil to make a hole in the middle of the pot. Then push the sharp end of the pencil through the hole.

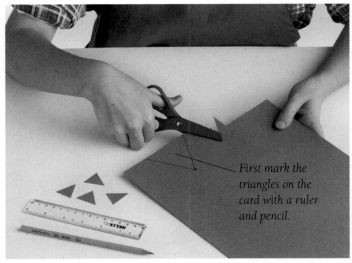

*First mark the triangles on the card with a ruler and pencil.*

**2.** Draw four small triangles and two large triangles on the coloured card. Carefully cut them out with the scissors.

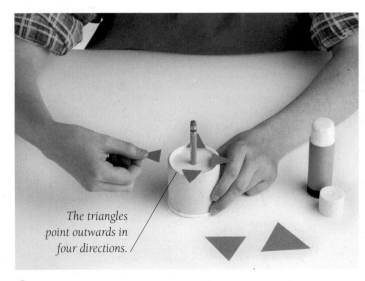

*The triangles point outwards in four directions.*

**3.** Glue each of the four small triangles to the plastic pot. Look at the picture to see where they should go. These will show the direction of the wind.

*Push the base of the other triangle into the straw to make the vane's pointer.*

*Push the pointed end of one triangle into the straw to make the wind vane's tail.*

**4.** Cut a short slit at either end of the straw. Insert the two large triangles into the slits to make an arrow-shaped pointer. This is called a "vane".

*Make sure that the vane spins easily.*

*Press the pot firmly into the clay.*

*The clay holds the wind vane steady.*

**5.** Carefully push the drawing pin right through the centre of the straw. Then push it into the rubber on the pencil end.

**6.** Make a ring of modelling clay and push the pot firmly into it, so it cannot blow away. Your wind vane is ready to use.

**Whirling in the wind**

As well as finding out the direction of the wind, it is also important to measure the speed of the wind. High-speed winds may cause damage and may be dangerous to ships and aircraft. The instrument shown below is called an anemometer. It measures the speed of the wind. The moving air makes the cups whirl round and the wind speed shows on the scale. There is a scale to describe wind strength. It ranges from 0 (calm) to 12 (a hurricane).

*The wind spins the cups.*

*The wind speed is shown on the dial.*

*The direction of the wind is the direction from which it comes.*

West

North

*Position the wind vane so that the triangles point north, east, south, and west. Use a compass to help you.*

South

East

*In a south wind, the vane points to the south.*

**7.** Place your wind vane outside. The vane swings around in the direction of the wind.

# WATER AND LIQUIDS

**Building with water**
A snowman is made with solid water! Snowflakes consist of ice. They are made up of ice crystals that form in clouds in cold weather.

Water is wonderful. You can have fun swimming and playing in water. Rain is not so much fun, but we could not live without it. It brings us the water we need to drink and to grow crops for food. Water is a "liquid", which is a substance that flows easily. There are many other liquids. Oil, such as cooking oil, is another. When liquids are cooled, they turn to solids. Water freezes to become hard ice. Heating water turns it into a gas called "water vapour", which disappears into the air. When water vapour cools, it turns back to liquid water.

**Water for life**
People, animals, and plants all need water to live. Water helps keep your body working, so that you stay alive.

**World of water**
This photograph of the Earth shows the blue oceans and the white clouds that bring rain. The brown land with no clouds is a huge desert where no rain falls.

**The power of water**
Water can change the shape of the land. Waves battering the shore wear away the rocks. Rain washes soil into rivers, which carry it away.

**Mostly water**
There is as much water in these buckets as in the girl's body! More than half of your body is water.

# 10 Measure the rain

Rain falls from the clouds, which contain millions of tiny water droplets. These come together, forming raindrops that fall to the ground. Make a simple rain gauge to measure "rainfall". This is the amount of rain that falls over a certain time.

**You will need:**

Ruler and marker pen

Measuring jug

Small, clear plastic bottle

Scissors

Large, clear plastic bottle

**1.** 🏃 Cut off the tops of both bottles, using the scissors. Make sure the edges are straight.

**2.** Fill the jug to the 50 ml mark. Pour the water into the small bottle. Mark the level.

**3.** Repeat step 2 several times, so that you have a series of marks on the side of the bottle.

**4.** Empty the small bottle. Place it inside the large bottle. Put the top of the large bottle upside-down over the small bottle. It forms a funnel.

*Empty the bottle after measuring the rainfall. Put it back in the same place.*

**5.** Stand the bottles outside on a table or a wall to catch the rain. Record the water level in the small bottle each morning. This is the daily rainfall.

Chart showing the rainfall for 12 months

Rainfall in mm

**6.** Add up the rainfall for each week or each month. Then make a chart to show how much rain falls over several weeks, months, or even a whole year.

### Weather station
Every day, scientists called meteorologists take detailed measurements to help them keep track of the weather and forecast how it will change. They record the amount of rainfall, the highest and lowest temperatures, the humidity, the speed and direction of the wind, and the air pressure.

# 11 Rain-test materials

Use rainwater to discover the water resistance of different materials. You will soon see why only certain materials are used with water.

**You will need:**

Cotton, paper, felt, rubber, plastic

Pen

Elastic bands

Scissors

Five jars

Waterproof paints

Paintbrush

**1.** 👫 Draw a circle that's wider than the top of the jar. Cut it out.

**2.** Place the circle of material over the top of one jar. Secure it to the jar with an elastic band.

**3.** Paint a face on the jar. Repeat steps one to three with the remaining four pieces of material and jars.

*Wool holds water longer than cotton, but is not waterproof.*

*Cotton is not waterproof and lets in water.*

*Plastic is waterproof and so is used to make things that hold water.*

*Rubber is waterproof and stretchy so is used to make swimming caps.*

*Paper is not at all waterproof and it falls apart in the rain.*

**4.** Place your five finished jars in the rain. Leave them for two hours before looking at them again. Make notes on what you find.

**Coated materials**
Materials can be made water-resistant by coating them with a waterproof material, such as rubber or wax. Some umbrella canopies are made from plastic, but others have nylon canopies coated with water-resistant chemicals.

# 12 Have fun with water pressure

Have fun finding out how water pressure can splash a stream of water over a distance. Fountains use water pressure to shoot water at different heights.

**You will need:**

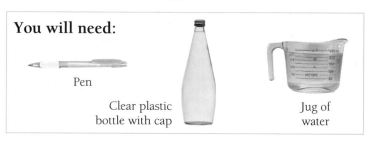

Pen

Clear plastic bottle with cap

Jug of water

**1.** 👥 Fill the bottle with water, replace the cap tightly, and lie the bottle on its side. Make a small hole halfway down with a pen.

**2.** Hold the bottle upright. Find a friend to surprise. Unscrew the lid and the water will spurt out of the hole!

*The water will flow out of the hole only when the cap is removed because it needs air to release the pressure.*

# 13 Remove a lime's lifejacket

Buoyancy is a force that pushes up from the water. A lifejacket filled with air pushes on water with a weaker force than it receives from the water, so it increases buoyancy and helps you to float.

**You will need:**

Lime

Peeler

Clear, tall glass of water

**1.** Place a lime into the glass of water. The fruit will float.

**2.** 👥 Peel the lime and place the fruit back in the glass. This time the lime sinks.

*The lime's rind is filled with tiny bubbles that make it float, just like a lifejacket.*

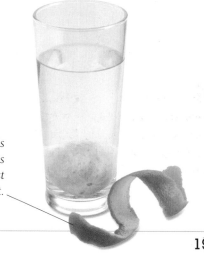

# 14 Make things sink, then float!

A huge ship floats on water, even though it is very heavy. Yet a small, light object such as a marble sinks! The weight of the objects does not matter. Whether or not something floats depends on how much water it "displaces", or pushes aside.

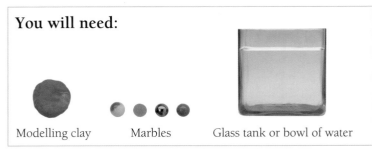

**You will need:**

Modelling clay    Marbles    Glass tank or bowl of water

**1.** Drop marbles into the water. They quickly sink to the bottom. Roll the clay into a ball.

*The displaced water pushes on the objects, but not enough to make them float.*

**2.** The clay ball also sinks. Like the marbles, it does not displace much water.

**3.** Remove the marbles and the clay ball. Shape the clay to make a boat.

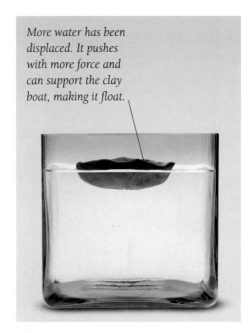

*More water has been displaced. It pushes with more force and can support the clay boat, making it float.*

**4.** Now the clay floats! The boat is bigger than the ball was and displaces more water.

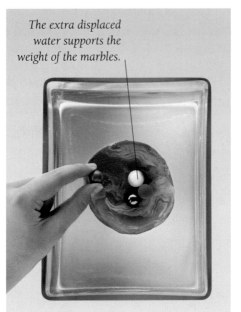

*The extra displaced water supports the weight of the marbles.*

**5.** Add a cargo of marbles. The boat settles lower, but displaces more water and still floats.

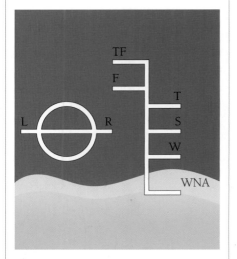

TF
F
T
L    R    S
W
WNA

**Safety level**
An overloaded ship settles too low in the water and could sink. Marks on a ship's side show safe loading levels.

# 15 Find out about floating

An object floats in water if it displaces enough water. But how much water is "enough"? Find out by collecting the displaced water and weighing it. It always weighs the same as the floating object.

Kitchen scales · Jug of water · Big glass jar · Small glass jar · Large dish

*Fill the jar to the brim.*

**1.** Remove the pan from the scales and reset the scales to zero. Put the scales in the dish. Rest the big jar on the scales and fill it with water. Note its weight.

**2.** Float the small jar in the big jar. It displaces water, which spills out into the dish. The weight of the big jar does not change.

**3.** Carefully remove the big jar and the dish. Put the pan on the scales and adjust them to zero. Pour in the water that had spilled into the dish.

## Afloat like a boat

When you float in water, your body displaces water, like any other floating object. The displaced water weighs as much as you do. It pushes up against your body and supports it so you do not sink.

**4.** Write down the weight of the water in the pan. Remove the pan and reset the scales to zero.

**5.** Now weigh the small jar that was floating in the big jar. You can see that it has the same weight as the water it displaced.

# 16 Command a deep-sea diver

At your command, a toy diver will dive into a bottle of water and then return to the surface. The diver you make works in the same way as submarines and other vessels that can dive deep under the sea.

**You will need:**

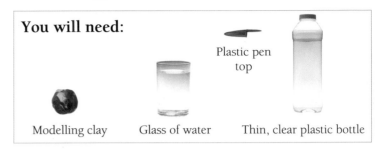

Plastic pen top

Modelling clay · Glass of water · Thin, clear plastic bottle

*If there is a hole in the tip, seal it with clay.*

**1.** Make your toy diver by sticking a small piece of clay to the pen top.

*Only the tip should be above the water.*

**2.** Put the diver in a glass of water. Add or remove clay until it only just floats.

*A bubble of air is trapped inside the pen top. This makes it float.*

**3.** Fill the bottle to the top with water. Put the diver in and screw the top on tightly.

*Water enters the pen top. The bubble gets smaller, and no longer supports the pen top.*

**4.** Squeeze the sides of the bottle. The diver sinks to the bottom!

*Water leaves the pen top. The air bubble gets bigger again and makes the pen top float once more.*

**5.** Stop squeezing and release your grip on the bottle. Now the diver rises back to the top.

**Down in the depths**

This underwater vessel explores the ocean depths. It has tanks that are flooded with water to make it dive. To make it rise to the surface again, air is pumped into these tanks. This drives out the water, and the vessel floats.

# 17 Make an underwater volcano

Did you know that you can get water to float on water? Hot water always rises to the surface and floats on cold water underneath it. Show this happening by making a "volcano" erupt under water and send up a huge plume of "smoke".

**You will need:**

Scissors    Paintbrush

Small bottle    Hot and cold water    Red food colouring    String    Large glass jar

**1.** Cut a long piece of string. Tie one end firmly around the neck of the bottle.

**2.** Tie the other end of the piece of string around the neck of the bottle to make a loop.

**3.** Pour cold water into the large glass jar until it is about three-quarters full.

**4.** Fill the bottle with hot water. Add food colouring to turn the water bright red.

**5.** Hold the bottle by the loop of string. Lower it gently into the jar of cold water.

**6.** The hot red water rises from the bottle like smoke from an erupting volcano.

**Hot-water holes**
There are deep holes in the ocean floor. Water, heated by the hot rocks deep in the Earth's crust, shoots out of these holes and rises to the surface of the sea. Divers have discovered strange sea creatures that live around these hot-water holes.

# 18 See how liquids float and sink

Liquids can float and sink just as solid objects can. It all depends on something called "density". A substance with a lower density weighs less than the same volume of one with a higher density. An object or liquid will float only in a liquid more dense than itself.

**You will need:**

Syrup

Vegetable oil

Coloured water

Selection of objects to float

Large container

**1.** Carefully pour syrup into the container until it is a quarter full. It is easier if you pour the syrup over the back of a spoon.

**2.** Slowly pour the same amount of vegetable oil into the container. Then add the same amount of coloured water.

**3.** The three liquids separate into three layers and float on each other. Now add the objects you plan to try to float.

**4.** The objects float at different levels. They sink until they reach a liquid of a higher density than themselves. They float on that liquid.

*Water is more dense than the oil but less dense than the syrup.*

*The grape is more dense than the water but less dense than the syrup.*

**Liquid tester**
A lump of modelling clay on a straw makes a "hydrometer", which measures density. The level at which it floats depends on a liquid's density. The denser the liquid, the higher it floats.

# 19 Find out if liquids mix

It is easy to colour some liquids, but not others. See how oil "resists" being tinted with food colouring. This means it does not let the colouring mix into it, and the colour cannot spread through oil. Find out what then happens to the colour in water.

**You will need:**

Food colouring · Glass beaker · Spoon · Dropper · Water jug · Coolking oil

**1.** Pour some water into the beaker, then add some oil. They form two separate layers because oil and water do not mix.

**2.** Carefully add a few drops of food colouring to the beaker. Use a dropper if necessary. The drops float about in the oil.

**3.** Using a spoon, push the drops of food colouring into the water. The colour bursts out as the drops meet the water and mix with it.

# 20 Test the flow of liquids

It takes much longer to pour syrup into a glass than to pour water. This is because the syrup has a high "viscosity". This means it does not flow easily. Test the viscosities of different liquids. The ones in this experiment should be easy to find.

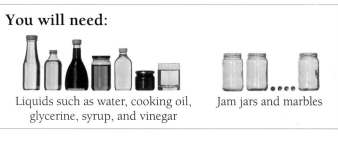

**You will need:**

Liquids such as water, cooking oil, glycerine, syrup, and vinegar · Jam jars and marbles

**1.** Fill the jars with different liquids. Drop a marble into each one.

**2.** The slower the marble falls, the higher the viscosity of the liquid.

# 21 Grow a stalactite

Stalactites are long thin columns of minerals hanging from the roofs of caves. They form over many centuries as the water drips and deposits the minerals. But you can grow one in less than a week!

**You will need:**

Paperclips • Spoon

Short length of wool • Jug of warm water • Plate • Two jars • Washing soda

**1.** Fill both the jars with warm water. Add washing soda and stir until no more soda dissolves.

**2.** Attach a paperclip to each end of the wool. Place the ends in the jars, so the wool hangs between the jars.

*Washing soda solution*

*The soda solution flows along the wool.*

*Washing soda solution*

*Drip of soda solution*

*The stalactite grows as each drip evaporates and leaves a little soda behind.*

*More crystals form in plate.*

**3.** Place a plate between the jars to catch the drips. Leave the jars for several days. A white stalactite grows down from the wool. A stalagmite grows up from the plate.

## Stalactites

Water flowing underground dissolves minerals as it seeps through rocks. It then deposits the minerals as stalactites when it drips through a cave roof. Water falling from the end of a stalactite builds up a column of minerals on the floor called a stalagmite. The stalactite and stalagmite may eventually meet to form a pillar.

# 22 Is water hard?

Water can be "hard", but not hard like rock. If tap water is hard, it builds up a deposit of minerals inside pipes and kettles. Soap does not easily form bubbles in hard water. Find out if the water from the taps in your house is hard.

**You will need:**

Spoon     Dropper

 Tap water

Two screw-top jars

Small open jar

Distilled water

Liquid soap

**1.** Mix liquid soap with some distilled water in the small jar. Distilled water is not hard.

**2.** Pour distilled water into one screw-top jar, and the same amount of tap water into the other.

**3.** Put a drop of liquid soap solution into the jar of tap water. Screw on the lid.

**4.** Shake the jar. If it does not foam, repeat step 3 and shake it again. Count how many drops you need to make the water foam.

*If the tap water needs more drops to make it foam than the distilled water, it is hard.*

### Water softening
Hard water builds up scaly mineral deposits in kettles and pipes. It can be softened by passing it through a filter that uses chemicals to remove the minerals from the water.

**5.** Repeat steps 3 and 4 with the distilled water. Did the tap water need more drops to make it foam?

# 23 Race a speedboat

Make a paper boat race across a bowl – just by touching the surface of the water! This happens because there is a strong force there, called "surface tension".

**You will need:**

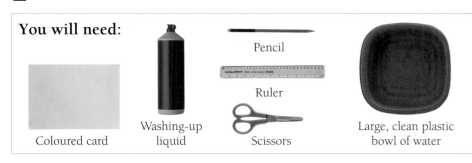

Coloured card

Washing-up liquid

Pencil

Ruler

Scissors

Large, clean plastic bowl of water

**1.** Draw the shape of your boat on the card. This one has a triangular shape.

**2.** Carefully cut out your boat shape. Then put it on the water and let it float.

**3.** Squeeze a small drop of the washing-up liquid on your finger.

**4.** Dip your finger in the water, just behind the boat. The boat shoots forwards across the bowl.

*The washing-up liquid weakens the surface tension behind the boat.*

*You must change the water in the bowl if you want to try again.*

*The surface tension is stronger in front of the boat. This pulls the boat forwards.*

**Make metal float**
Gently place a paperclip on the water's surface, and it will float! The surface tension of the water is strong enough to support very light objects, such as paperclips.

# 24 See plants drinking

Plants need water to live, just as you do. By making some flowers change colour, you can see how water moves upwards. It flows through a plant's stem and into its leaves and flowers.

**You will need:**

Four glasses

Different coloured inks or food colouring

Fresh white flowers

Scissors

**1.** Pour a little food colouring or ink into each glass. Then add some water.

**2.** 👤 Trim the stems of the flowers. Split part of the stem of one flower in two.

**3.** Put a flower in each glass of coloured water. The split stem goes in two glasses.

**4.** Leave the flowers in a warm room. Very slowly, they change colour.

**Thirsty leaves**
Place a twig with leaves on it in a glass of water. Add some cooking oil, and mark a scale on the glass. Observe this for a few days to see how the level of the water falls as the leaves suck up the water. The layer of oil on the water stops it evaporating, so you can be sure all the water that has gone from the glass has been absorbed by the plant.

*Green flower*

*Red flower*

*Red water travels up the stem to the petals, staining them red.*

*Each part of the split stem feeds different coloured water into the flower.*

**5.** Each half of the flower with the split stem turns a different colour. One half of the split stem feeds red water into it and the other half feeds blue water.

*Red and green flower*

# HOT AND COLD

Something that is hot, like a hot drink, feels very different from something cold, like ice cream. But both sensations are caused by the same thing – heat. The difference is that cold objects contain less heat than hot ones. Our bodies make heat from our food. We also get heat from the Sun and from burning fuels.

**How hot?**
A thermometer measures the "temperature", which is how hot or cold something is. Temperature uses units called "degrees". This thermometer is showing a temperature of 36.6 degrees.

**Fire and flames**
Heating some materials makes them catch fire. This has happened to the trees in this forest. The flames of the fire produce heat, so that more material starts to burn and the fire spreads.

**A ball of fire**
The Sun is a huge ball of very hot gas. It glows with light and creates vast amounts of heat in the form of invisible heat rays. These travel through space and warm the Earth.

**Staying warm**
You wear thick clothes in cold weather. These keep you warm because they stop heat escaping from your body.

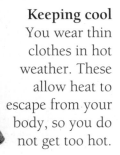

**Keeping cool**
You wear thin clothes in hot weather. These allow heat to escape from your body, so you do not get too hot.

# 25 Build a simple thermometer

A thermometer usually has a thin tube of coloured liquid. This liquid moves up and down inside the tube. The tube is marked with a scale showing degrees. The level of the liquid in the tube indicates the temperature.

**You will need:**

Clear straw

Card    Scissors    Cold water    Food colouring    Colouring pens    Glass bottle    Modelling clay

**1.** Pour cold water into the bottle until it is about three-quarters full. Add a few drops of food colouring.

*The seal must be airtight.*

**2.** Put a straw in the bottle so that it dips in the water. Seal around it with modelling clay.

**3.** Blow gently into the straw. The water rises up it. Stop when it is halfway up.

*The black mark shows a normal temperature.*

**4.** Cut two slits in the card. Slide it over the straw. Make a black mark to show the level of the water.

*The red mark shows a high (warm) temperature.*

*Heat makes the air inside the bottle expand and push the water up the straw.*

**5.** Put the thermometer in a warm place. The water rises. Mark the level in red.

*The blue mark shows a low (cool) temperature.*

*The air inside the bottle contracts as it cools, sucking the water back down the straw.*

**6.** Put the thermometer in a refrigerator for a while. The water level falls. Mark it in blue.

#  Race some beads

Heat spreads better through some materials than others. Show how well some common materials "conduct" heat, or let it spread through them. Good conductors take in most heat.

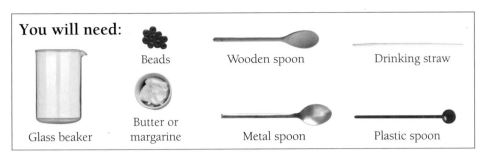

**You will need:**

Beads    Wooden spoon    Drinking straw

Glass beaker    Butter or margarine    Metal spoon    Plastic spoon

**1.** Use butter to stick one bead to each of the spoons and to the straw. Stand them in the beaker.

**2.**  Pour in hot water. Heat moves up the spoons and straw and melts the butter. See which bead falls first. It is stuck to the best conductor.

# 27 Circulate some heat

Show how heat moves around a liquid. This movement is called "convection". It happens in air, too. When you put a heater on in a room, its heat spreads by convection.

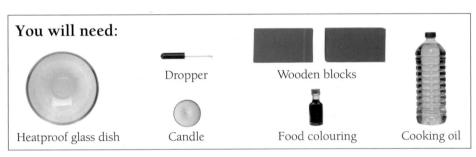

**You will need:**

Dropper    Wooden blocks

Heatproof glass dish    Candle    Food colouring    Cooking oil

**1.** Put the candle between the blocks. Ask an adult to light the candle.

**2.** Pour cooking oil into the dish and place it on the blocks. Put drops of food colouring at the bottom.

*The oil at the surface cools and sinks back to the bottom.*

**3.** Warm currents circulate in the oil. They carry drops of food colouring with them.

*As the oil gets hotter, it rises.*

*Drops of food colouring*

# 28 Keep a drink cool

When a liquid evaporates and changes into a gas, it takes in heat from its surroundings. Refrigerators use this principle to keep things cool. Try making your own refrigerator.

## You will need:

Two cans of drink    Glass dish    Jug of water    Flowerpot    Plant spray gun

*This can will warm up in the Sun's rays.*

*This can will stay cool during the experiment.*

**1.** Do this experiment on a sunny day. Take two cans of drink. Place one in the sunshine, and the other in a glass dish.

**2.** Cover the can in the dish with a flowerpot. Pour cold water over the flowerpot until it is fully soaked.

**3.** Leave the flowerpot to stand in sunshine. Spray it with water now and again to prevent it from drying out.

*As the water evaporates from the wet flowerpot, it takes heat from inside the flowerpot. This draws heat from the can and keeps the drink cool.*

**4.** After about an hour, take both cans and taste the drink from each one.

### Shivering swimmers

It is quite common to shiver soon after emerging from the sea or a pool, even if the weather is not particularly cold. As the water evaporates from your wet skin and costume, it draws heat from your body, making you feel cold. It is good to have a towel ready to wrap yourself in!

**5.** You will notice that the drink from the can that has been exposed to the Sun is the warmest. The wet flowerpot acts like a refrigerator and keeps the other drink cool.

# 29 Store some heat

Hot drinks lose heat easily, so they soon cool down. Make a heat store and keep some warm water in it. The store helps stop heat escaping, so the water inside it stays warmer for much longer.

**You will need:**

Sticky tape    Wide cork

Big jar with lid    Small jar with lid    Small glass    Warm water    Aluminium foil    Scissors

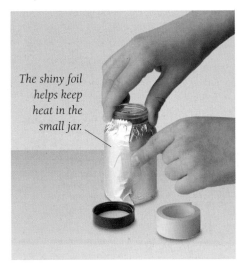

*The shiny foil helps keep heat in the small jar.*

**1.** Wrap two layers of foil tightly around the small jar, with the shiny sides facing inwards. Fasten the foil with tape.

**2.** Pour warm water into the small jar and the glass. Put the lid on the jar.

*The lids stop the heat escaping upwards.*

*Heat leaves the sides and top of the glass.*

*Heat does not pass easily through the cork and the air in the large jar.*

**3.** Place the cork in the bottom of the big jar and stand the small jar on it. Put the lid on the big jar.

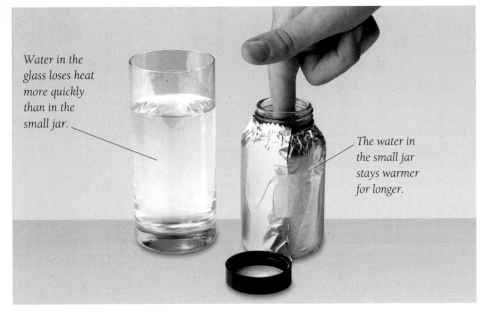

*Water in the glass loses heat more quickly than in the small jar.*

*The water in the small jar stays warmer for longer.*

**4.** After ten minutes, take out the small jar. The water in it is still warm, but the water in the glass has cooled.

**Heat barrier**

A vacuum flask keeps drinks hot or cold. It has two containers with tight lids, like your heat store. The inner container has shiny sides and a double wall with a "vacuum", or empty space, inside. It is so difficult for heat to leave or enter the flask that its contents stay hot, or remain cold, for a long time.

*Shiny sides*

*Liquid*

*Vacuum*

# 30 Fight a fire

Light a candle – and then put out the flame, as if by magic! This can be done because things burn only if they get oxygen gas from the air. Take away the supply of oxygen, and the fire goes out.

**You will need:**

Matches   Candle   Vinegar   Glass dish   Modelling clay   Spoon   Sodium bicarbonate

**1.** Using the modelling clay, stick the candle to the bottom of the dish.

*The top of the candle must be lower than the top of the dish.*

**2.** Sprinkle some sodium bicarbonate around the candle.

**3.** 👫 Ask an adult to light the candle with a match.

*The vinegar and the sodium bicarbonate release bubbles of carbon dioxide gas.*

*The froth must not reach the flame.*

*As the candle burns, it takes in oxygen from the air.*

**4.** Add some vinegar. The sodium bicarbonate begins to froth.

*Invisible carbon dioxide fills the glass and covers the flame. It cuts off the oxygen supply.*

**5.** Keep still and wait. Suddenly, the flame goes out, but you cannot see why.

*The match goes out as it enters the carbon dioxide.*

**6.** 👫 Try to light the candle again. It's impossible!

**Battling the flames**
Firefighters cover a fire with a layer of water, foam, or carbon dioxide. This layer stops air from reaching the flames. To go on burning, the fire needs oxygen from the air. Without oxygen, the fire goes out.

# Slice some ice

Cut right through an ice cube – and leave it in one piece! You do not use a knife for this amazing trick. You just cut the ice with a piece of wire.

### You will need:

Steel fork     Thin wire     Plastic bottle of water

Aluminium foil     Sticky tape     Ice cube     Heavy book

*Make sure the fork cannot move.*

**1.** Tape the fork to the table edge. Put the book on the handle.

*Knot the ends of the wire tightly together.*

**2.** Make a loop of wire and fix it firmly to the bottle.

**3.** Place the ice cube and a square of foil on the fork.

**4.** Put the wire over the ice cube. The weight of the bottle pulls the wire into the ice.

**5.** Slowly, the wire cuts right through the ice cube.

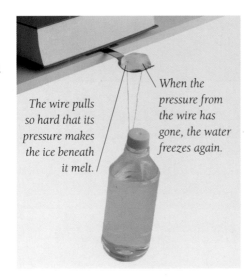

*The wire pulls so hard that its pressure makes the ice beneath it melt.*

*When the pressure from the wire has gone, the water freezes again.*

### Speed on the ice

Skaters can skim quickly over the ice. Their weight causes a film of water to form just beneath the blades of their skates. The skates slide easily along on this slippery film. The blades are slightly curved at the bottom so they grip the ice, even when at an angle.

**6.** Pick up the cube after the wire has passed right through it. The cube is still all in one piece!

# 32 Make your own ice cream

Make some tasty ice cream and find out how to make things freeze without putting them in the freezer. This is an old-fashioned way of making ice cream. It still works well.

**You will need:**

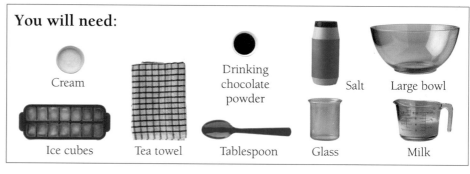

Cream

Ice cubes

Tea towel

Drinking chocolate powder

Tablespoon

Salt

Glass

Large bowl

Milk

**1.** Mix one spoon of chocolate, two spoons of milk, and one spoon of cream in the glass.

**2.** Put some ice cubes in the bowl and sprinkle a lot of salt over them.

**3.** Place the glass of ice-cream mixture in the large bowl, on top of the salted ice cubes.

*When salt is mixed with ice, it makes the ice melt. It also makes it colder.*

**4.** Build up more layers of ice cubes and salt around the glass.

*The ice needs heat to melt. It takes this from the ice-cream mixture, which gets so cold that it freezes.*

*The towel helps stop heat getting into the bowl from outside.*

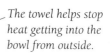

**5.** Place the tea towel over the bowl. Leave the ice-cream mixture to set for an hour. Stir it every few minutes.

### Spikes of ice
Icicles form where water drips over the edge of a cold surface. The cold surface draws heat from the water, which turns to ice. An icicle begins to form. As more water runs down the ice and freezes, the icicle grows.

**6.** Take the glass out of the bowl, and taste your home-made chocolate ice cream.

# LIGHT

Light makes it possible for you to see the world around you. Sources of light, such as the Sun and light bulbs, produce light rays. These bounce off objects, like this book. The rays then enter your eyes, and you see the objects. We use light to form "images" or pictures of things.

**Too small to be seen?**
You can see very tiny objects or creatures with a microscope. The image you see is highly "magnified", or much bigger than the actual object or creature.

**Broken and bent?**
The pen standing in this glass of water is in fact straight. It looks strange because water bends the light rays coming from the pen to your eyes.

**Mirror images**
You can see images of things in mirrors. The curved mirrors at the front and back form large and small images.

**Quick as a flash**
This camera makes a bright flash to give enough light to take a photograph. The light travels from the camera to the girl in two billionths of a second.

# 33 Play with shadows

Scare your friends by casting some spooky shadows on the wall! This will also show you how light travels in straight lines. Shadows form when an object blocks the light.

**You will need:**

Scissors · Pencil · Sticky tape · Thin card · Thin sticks · Bright torch · Tracing paper

**1.** Trace patterns of ghosts from a book, or invent some of your own and make drawings of them.

**2.** Transfer your ghost patterns from the tracing paper to the pieces of thin card.

**3.** 🧍 Carefully cut out the ghost patterns and tape each one to the end of a stick.

*The shadow forms where the rays are blocked by card and cannot reach the wall.*

*The shadow has the same shape as the card because the rays of light are straight and cannot bend around the edges of the card.*

*Rays of light come from the torch and light up the wall.*

**4.** Hold the patterns near the wall. Shine a torch on them, and large shadows of the ghosts appear on the wall!

**Sunny time**
You can tell the time with a sundial. The Sun casts a shadow of a tilted bar on to a set of lines, which mark the hours. Throughout the day, the shadow moves as the Sun travels across the sky. The position of the shadow on the lines gives the time.

# 34 Look around corners

Build a periscope. You can use it to see over walls or people's heads, and to peep around corners. A periscope works by using mirrors to reflect rays of light.

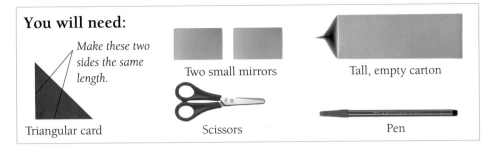

**You will need:**

*Make these two sides the same length.*

Triangular card

Two small mirrors

Tall, empty carton

Scissors

Pen

**1.** Use the triangular card to help you draw two diagonal lines on one side of the carton.

**2.** Carefully cut a slot along each line. The slots should be just wide enough for the mirrors to fit into.

**3.** Draw and cut two more slots on the other side of the carton.

*These slots must be directly opposite the first slots.*

**4.** Carefully push the mirrors into the slots. They should fit snugly, so they cannot slide out of the carton.

*The shiny side of the top mirror faces downwards.*

*The shiny side of the bottom mirror faces upwards.*

**5.** 👫 Draw a large square at the top of the carton in front of the mirror. Carefully cut it out.

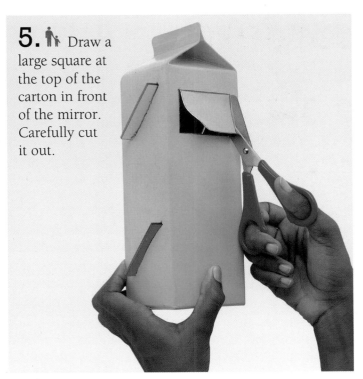

**6.** Make a small hole with a pencil in the back of the carton. Now your periscope is ready.

*Make the hole at the bottom, level with the mirror.*

**7.** Look into the hole to see around corners or over obstacles.

*Light rays enter through the square. They reflect from the top mirror to the bottom one.*

*The bottom mirror reflects the light rays so that they can enter your eye. You see an image of the scene at the level of the top mirror.*

### What's up there?

When a submarine is under water, the crew may want to see above the waves. They may need to find out if there are any ships nearby. They raise a periscope to the surface of the sea and look around. The periscope has a long tube that reflects light rays from above the surface of the water down to the submarine. A member of the crew looks into it to see what is going on above the submarine. The periscope may then be brought back down again.

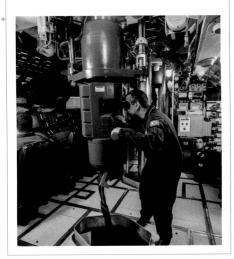

# 35 Build a kaleidoscope

Use mirrors and beads to make a colourful kaleidoscope. All you have to do is shake it, and beautiful patterns form, one after another.

**You will need:**

Sharp pencil

Torch

Sticky tape

Beads

Scissors

Card and tracing paper

Three small mirrors

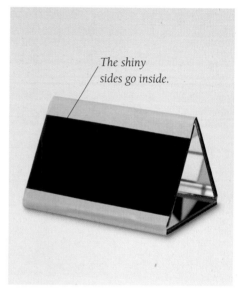

*The shiny sides go inside.*

**1.** Tape the three mirrors together to form a triangle.

**2.** Draw around the mirrors on the card.

**3.** Cut out the triangle. Use a pencil to make a hole in the middle of it.

**4.** Tape the triangle to one end of the mirrors.

**5.** Stretch the tracing paper over the other end of the mirrors. Tape it firmly in place.

**6.** Drop some beads through the hole. Your kaleidoscope is now ready.

**7.** Shine the torch onto the tracing paper, and look through the hole, into the kaleidoscope. You see several images of the beads combined, forming a pattern. Shake the kaleidoscope to change the pattern.

*The mirrors reflect light from the beads to form several images of them.*

**You, you, you, you, you...**
You can see many images in two parallel mirrors. This is because they keep reflecting light rays between them.

## 36 See double

Use water to turn one button into two! This trick depends on the way rays of light bend as they enter and leave water and glass. This bending of light rays is called "refraction". Refraction also makes a straight ruler look bent when it is standing in water.

**You will need:**

Glass       Jug of water       Button

*The button must not float.*

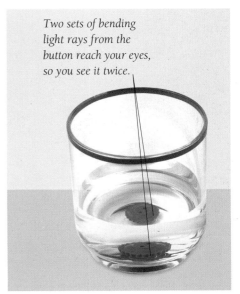

*Two sets of bending light rays from the button reach your eyes, so you see it twice.*

**1.** Put the button into the glass. Try to get it to lie right in the middle of the glass.

**2.** Gently pour some water into the glass until it is half full.

**3.** Look down at the glass from one side. It looks as if there are two buttons in the glass!

# 37 Make your own torch

We need light to drive out darkness – and we use electricity to make that light. Without electricity, we would have no proper light in our homes or streets. You can carry your own source of light with you if you have a torch. Press the switch, and a beam of light cuts through the darkness. Batteries in the torch provide the electricity it needs.

**You will need:**

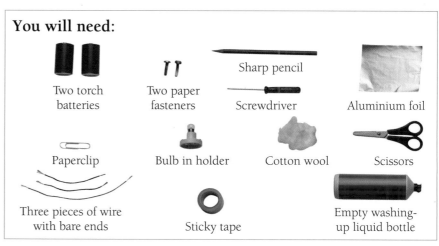

Two torch batteries

Two paper fasteners

Sharp pencil

Screwdriver

Aluminium foil

Paperclip

Bulb in holder

Cotton wool

Scissors

Three pieces of wire with bare ends

Sticky tape

Empty washing-up liquid bottle

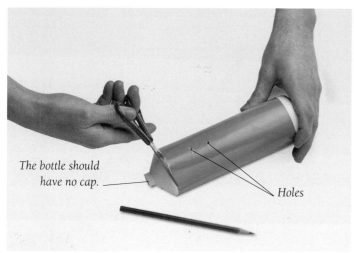

*The bottle should have no cap.*

*Holes*

**1.** Cut off the top of the bottle. Using the pencil, make two small holes in the side.

**2.** Tape foil to the inside of the bottle top. Make sure the shiny side faces outwards.

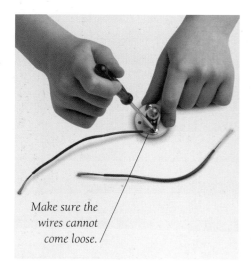

*Make sure the wires cannot come loose.*

**3.** Using the screwdriver, fix two of the pieces of wire firmly to the bulb-holder.

*Tape the top of one battery to the base of the other.*

**4.** Tape the batteries together. Then tape the third piece of wire to the lower battery.

**5.** Tape one of the wires from the bulb-holder to the terminal on the top battery.

*Fit cotton wool around the batteries to hold them firmly in place.*

**6.** Thread the wire from the bottom battery through the lower hole. Pack cotton wool into the bottle and insert the batteries.

**7.** Thread the wire from the bulb-holder through the top hole in the bottle. Fix both wires to paper fasteners, and push in the fasteners.

**8.** Place the bulb-holder on the batteries and tape the centre of the bottle top over the bulb.

**9.** Bend the paperclip and fit one end under the lower paper fastener. This is the switch.

*Closing the switch lets electricity flow from the batteries along the wires to the bulb.*

**Bright bulb**
A light-emitting diode, also known as LED, creates light by electroluminescence, which means it lights up when electricity passes through it. When an LED is switched on, electricity activates tiny particles called electrons inside the bulb. As they move, they release energy as bright light.

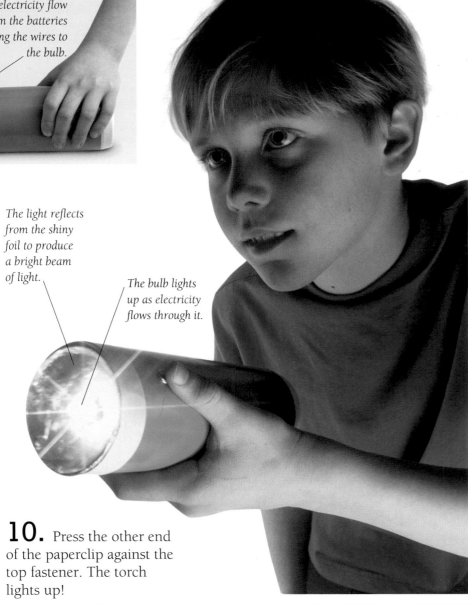

*The light reflects from the shiny foil to produce a bright beam of light.*

*The bulb lights up as electricity flows through it.*

**10.** Press the other end of the paperclip against the top fastener. The torch lights up!

# 38 Construct a camera

Build a model of a simple camera, to show how it works. Your model camera uses a magnifying glass to form a picture, just as the lens in a real camera does.

**You will need:**

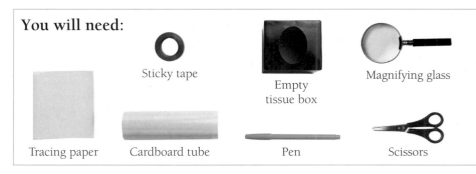

Sticky tape

Empty tissue box

Magnifying glass

Tracing paper

Cardboard tube

Pen

Scissors

**1.** Hold the tube on the side of the box opposite the opening. Draw around it.

**2.** 👫 Carefully cut out the circle you have drawn on the tissue box.

**3.** Push the tube into the hole. The tube should move in and out.

**4.** Tape the magnifying glass firmly to the end of the tube.

**5.** Tape the tracing paper over the opening in the box. Now you can use your model camera.

## Taking photographs

A real camera has a lens like the magnifying glass, and a memory card in place of the tracing paper. When you take a photograph, light passes through the lens and forms an image upside-down, which is recorded on the memory card. You can view this image on your camera's screen or on your computer.

*The magnifying glass is a lens. It makes the rays of light from the flowers bend and meet on the paper.*

**6.** Point the camera at a bright object. An image of it appears on the tracing paper.

*Move the tube in and out until the image is sharp.*

*An image forms where the rays of light meet. It is back to front and upside-down.*

# 39 Bend a beam of light

Light travels in straight lines, but its path can be altered by reflecting it off other surfaces. This experiment uses the reflective properties of water to bend the path of a light beam.

**You will need:**

Paintbrush

Black acrylic paint

Nail

Modelling clay

Pile of books

Bendy straw

Pliers

Torch

Jug of water

Plastic funnel

Glass dish

Clear plastic bottle

**1.** Paint one vertical half of the plastic bottle black and let it dry.

**2.** 👤 Ask an adult to make a hole about 6 cm (2.4 in) up from the base on the black side. A heated nail makes a neat, round hole, but it must be held with pliers.

**3.** Push the end of a bendy straw into the hole. Press modelling clay around the hole to prevent leakages. Plug the end of the straw with modelling clay.

**4.** Fill the bottle with water. Place it on a pile of books and position a glass dish underneath the straw.

*Light cannot escape the stream's sides and follows its path.*

*Light reflects back and forth between the stream's sides.*

**5.** Turn out the light. Shine a torch at the hole from the bottle's clear side. Remove the plug from the straw and put your finger under the stream of water. You will see a tiny spot of light dancing on your finger!

## Light messages

Telephone conversations and computer data are often sent along cables as pulses of light. Inside the cables, the light travels along very thin glass threads called optical fibres. The light bounces along the optical fibres as it reflects off the sides of the glass threads.

# COLOUR

Imagine a world without colour. It would be like living in an old black-and-white film! Colour helps to bring beauty to our world. There are beautiful colours in nature, and we use colour in our clothes and to decorate our homes. Colour is in the light that comes from objects. Red light comes from red objects, for example. We detect colour when the light enters our eyes.

**Colour codes**
We give colours certain meanings. In traffic lights, red means "stop" and green means "go", for example.

**Curve of colours**
A rainbow occurs when the Sun lights up a shower of rain. The rain drops turn the white sunlight into bands of colour. You can only see a rainbow if the Sun is shining behind you.

**Colours for camouflage**
Some animals, such as this green chameleon, have colours that match their surroundings. This makes it hard for other animals to spot them.

**Colourful creatures**
Many animals, like these beautiful butterflies, have bright colours. These colours may attract other animals or warn off enemies.

# 40 Make a rainbow

You can see a rainbow without having to wait for rain. "White" or colourless light is in fact a mixture of all colours of the rainbow. Water can split this light into these colours.

**You will need:**

Mirror   Jar of water   Modelling clay   Bright torch   Shallow dish   White card

**1.** Pour water into the shallow dish until it is about half full.

**2.** Put the mirror in the dish. Use modelling clay to fix it so that it slopes.

**3.** Shine the torch on the part of the mirror that is under the water.

*As the white light from the torch enters and leaves the water, it splits up into bands of colour.*

**4.** Hold the card above the dish. A rainbow appears on it! See how many different colours there are. You may have to move the card or torch before you can see the rainbow.

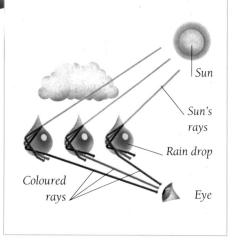

*The mirror reflects the light from the torch so that it strikes the card.*

**Inside a rainbow**

When you see a rainbow, you are seeing rays of light from the Sun. These rays of white light have been reflected by the drops of rain, which makes them split up into all the colours of the rainbow.

Sun

Sun's rays

Rain drop

Coloured rays

Eye

# 41 See a sunset

The Sun often goes a lovely orange or red when it sets at dusk. Find out why this happens by making your own sunset. You can do this using a torch and a glass of milky water.

**You will need:**

Milk          Glass beaker of water          Torch          Spoon

**1.** Shine the torch through the beaker of water. It looks white, like the Sun when it is high up in the sky.

**2.** Pour a little milk into the water in the beaker.

**3.** Stir the water gently, so that it all goes slightly white.

**4.** Shine the torch through the water again. Now the torch light looks orange-red, just like the setting Sun!

*Particles of milk in the water cut out some of the colours in the light coming from the torch. Only orange and red rays get through.*

**Rosy dawn and fiery dusk**
When the Sun is low in the sky, in the morning and evening, its light passes through more air than at other times of day. Tiny particles in the air stop much of the Sun's light. Only orange and red light gets through.

# 42 Discover hidden colours

Paper that can soak up water can separate colours from ink or food colouring. This is because it soaks up some colours faster than others. Find the hidden colours in dark liquids!

**You will need:**

Dropper · Paperclips

Coloured inks and food colouring · Blotting paper · Small jars · Narrow rod

**1.** In each jar, make a different mixture of inks and food colouring.

*The liquids go dark as the colours mix together.*

**2.** Tear the blotting paper into strips and fasten these to the rod. Place a drop of each mixture near the end of each paper strip.

*Red, orange, and blue* · *Green, yellow, and blue* · *Brown and blue* · *Blue, purple, and brown*

**3.** Clean out the jars, and pour a little clear water into each one. Lower the paper strips into the jars so that the ends just touch the water. The colours on each strip move up and separate out into different coloured bands.

**Making paints**

A pot of coloured paint contains more than one colour – the colours are hidden. Paints are made by mixing several different "pigments" or colouring materials together. Different mixtures give different shades.

# 43 Mix colours together

Pictures in books like this one can show all the colours of the rainbow. Yet only three colours and black are used to make them all. Show how you can mix two or three colours to make any colour you want.

**You will need:**

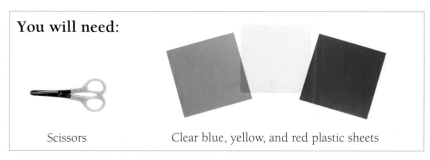

Scissors          Clear blue, yellow, and red plastic sheets

**1.** Cut the plastic sheets into several strips, all the same width.

**2.** Place yellow and blue strips on a white surface. Green appears where they overlap and the colours mix.

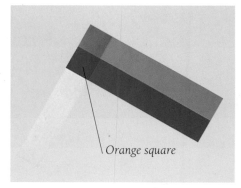

*Orange square*

**3.** Add a red strip to begin a pattern of squares. See how red and yellow mix to form orange.

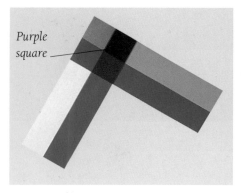

*Purple square*

**4.** Add another red strip to cross over the blue. Purple forms where the two colours mix.

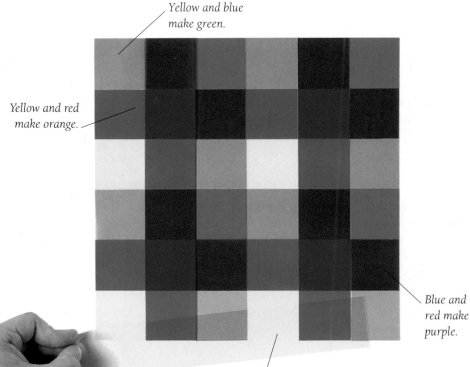

*Yellow and blue make green.*

*Yellow and red make orange.*

*Blue and red make purple.*

*Bright yellow, red or blue form where the same colours overlap.*

**5.** Add more strips. Red, blue, and yellow mix to form several different colours.

# 44 Spin some colours

Ordinary white light, such as sunlight, seems to have no colour, but it contains all the colours of the rainbow! Colour a disc and spin it to show this amazing fact.

**You will need:**

Violet, indigo, blue, green, yellow, orange and red paints

Protractor

Paint brushes

Sharp pencil

Water for paint

**1.** 👥 Cut out a disc of white card. Use the protractor to mark seven sections. Paint each one a different colour.

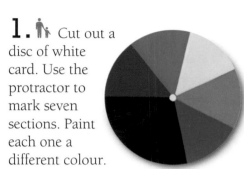

**2.** 👥 Make a hole in the centre of the disc. Push in the point of the pencil. Spin the disc. The colours disappear as they mix to form white!

*Slow spin*

*Fast spin*

# 45 Change colour

An object gets its colour by reflecting light. Instead of reflecting all the colours in light, it reflects only some. Show how this happens by using coloured cellophane to let only certain colours reach your eyes from an object.

**You will need:**

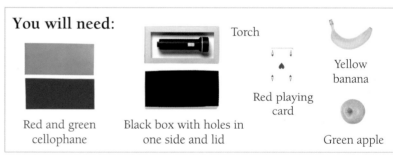

Torch

Red and green cellophane

Black box with holes in one side and lid

Red playing card

Yellow banana

Green apple

**1.** Put the objects in the box. Place green cellophane over the hole in the top and shine a torch through the side hole.

*The red hearts do not reflect green light, so they look black.*

*The yellow banana and green apple both reflect green light.*

Only green light passes through the cellophane.

**2.** Do the same thing again, this time with red cellophane. The red hearts disappear, while the green apple goes dark. The banana now looks red instead of yellow.

*The white card reflects all colours, so now it looks red.*

*The yellow banana reflects red as well as green light.*

*The green apple does not reflect red light.*

Only red light passes through the cellophane.

# 46 Test with colour

Make a liquid change colour suddenly, as if by magic! You can use this colour change as a test, to find out if a substance is an acid or an alkali – or neither of these.

**You will need:**

Saucepan          Large jar

Sieve          Red cabbage, knife, and chopping board          Spoons          Four small jars          Distilled or purified water

**1.** Carefully chop the red cabbage into small pieces.

**2.** Heat some distilled water in the saucepan. Add the cabbage.

**3.** Let the cabbage water cool, then strain it into the large jar.

**4.** Put cabbage water in the small jars and test various substances.

Lemon juice

Vinegar

Cream of tartar

**5.** Test lemon juice, vinegar, and cream of tartar. They are acids, which turn the cabbage water red.

Distilled water

**6.** Add distilled water to the cabbage water. It stays reddish purple. The distilled water is neither an acid nor an alkali.

### Colour varieties

Acids or alkalis in the soil make a difference to the colours of hydrangeas. They have blue flowers if they are growing in acid soil and pink ones if the soil is alkaline.

Sodium bicarbonate

Tap water

**7.** Test sodium bicarbonate. It is a weak alkali and turns the cabbage water blue. Tap water may do the same thing.

Ammonia

Washing soda

**8.** Test a little ammonia or washing soda. These strong alkalis turn the cabbage water green.

# 47 See colours in bubbles

Soap bubbles caught in the light look very colourful. This experiment shows you how to make amazing bubble colours and blow spectacular bubbles at the same time!

**You will need:**

Glycerol (glycerin)    Washing-up liquid    Torch    Straw    Half a litre of water    Plate    Spoon

**1.** Stir four spoons of washing-up liquid (not lemon) and one spoon of glycerol into half a litre of water.

**2.** Pour some of the solution on to a plate. Wet the end of a straw and put it in the solution. Gently blow through the other end to create a large bubble.

**3.** Carefully remove the straw from the bubble. Blow a second bubble beside the first one. Try to make sure that the bubbles are about the same size.

*Keep the torch beam level with the bubbles.*

**4.** Turn out the light and shine a torch at the bubbles. Point the torch beam at the "wall" that forms where the two bubbles meet.

**5.** View the wall between the bubbles from an angle. Beautiful coloured bands appear across the bubble wall! Adjust the position of the torch if you cannot see them at first.

*The glycerin in the solution makes the bubbles strong, so they last longer than normal.*

*Light from the torch reflects off both the front and back of the bubble wall. The two reflected beams of light mix, or "interfere", with each other, creating amazing coloured stripes.*

# 48 Print pretty patterns

Print some colourful and pretty patterns on paper. The colours transfer to the paper in the same way that they do when colour pictures are printed in books.

**You will need:**

Paintbrush

Palette

Linseed oil (or white spirit)

Thick paper

Poster paints

Dish of water

**1.** Put some poster paints on the palette.

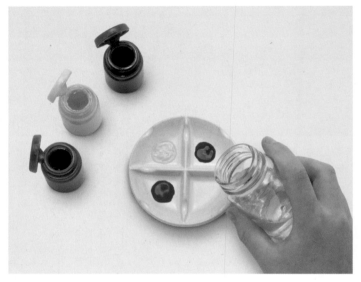

**2.** Mix a little white spirit or linseed oil with each colour on the palette.

**3.** Put one colour from the palette on the brush and gently add the paint to the water.

**4.** Add another colour. Swirl the colours with the brush to make a pattern.

**5.** Gently lay a sheet of the paper on the water, so that it lies on the surface.

**6.** Carefully peel the paper away from the water. Lift it out and lay it on a flat surface.

*Red and blue pattern*

*Yellow and blue pattern*

**7.** Let the paper dry. Try printing more patterns with other colours.

*Red and yellow pattern*

*The coloured oil does not mix with water, so it transfers to the paper.*

### Printing in colour

Colour printing presses have rollers on which pictures are formed with coloured inks. Paper passes through the rollers and the coloured ink transfers to the paper, making colour pictures.

# GROWTH

Living things are usually small when they start life. They grow and become adult. People and animals need food to make them grow. Plants grow, too, and they also need food. Most plants make their own food from air, water, and sunlight. They use this food to grow stems and leaves, and sometimes to bear flowers and fruits. The leaves and fruits may then become food for people and animals.

### Greatest growth
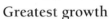
These trees are the biggest living things in the world. They are giant sequoias, which begin life as little seeds and can grow to 110 m (360 ft) tall.

### Plant products
Many useful things are made from plants – clothes from cotton, for example, and paper from trees.

### Bursting buds
Place some budding twigs in water. Soon, leaves and flowers will grow from the buds. These are horse chestnut twigs.

### Good food
Growing plants provide foods, such as these fruits and vegetables. Food products, such as bread and sugar, are also made from plants.

### Living parts
All living things are made of many tiny parts called cells. By looking at plants through a magnifying glass, you can see how they are formed. This is a magnified view of a moss plant.

# 49 Discover the needs of seeds

Seeds seem lifeless, but they can suddenly come alive and grow into plants. Show how they need three things for this – water, oxygen gas from the air, and warmth.

**You will need:**

Paper towels      Jug of water      Bowl of water

Mung bean seeds      Three deep saucers

**1.** Place the beans in the bowl of water and leave them to soak overnight.

**2.** Put paper towels in the saucers. You may need to fold them in two.

**3.** Pour a little water into the first saucer to moisten the towel.

**4.** Place some beans on the paper towel in each one of the three saucers.

**5.** Pour enough water into the second saucer to cover the beans.

*Keep the beans covered by adding more water every day.*

*The underwater beans begin to grow, but the water stops air getting to them and they stop growing.*

*Keep the paper moist by adding a little water when necessary.*

*The dry beans get no water and do not begin to grow.*

**6.** Leave the saucers in a warm place for several days. Only the beans in the first saucer begin to grow properly.

*These beans grow because they get water from the moist paper and oxygen from the air, and they are warm.*

## Growing crops

Farmers sow seeds of crop plants on the land. The seeds need water to start growing, and the young crops also need water to grow. If it does not rain, the seeds and plants must be given water. These crops are being sprayed with water. Watering crops is called "irrigation".

# 50 See how a plant grows

Most plants begin life beneath the ground. They grow from seeds, which drop into the soil. There is a way you can see what happens out of sight under the ground. A bean is the seed of a bean plant. You can grow it in a glass jar, where you can see it clearly.

**You will need:**

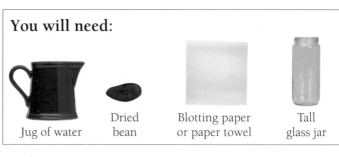

Jug of water   Dried bean   Blotting paper or paper towel   Tall glass jar

*Soak the bean in water for a day first.*

*Keep the paper moist by adding water when necessary.*

*The bean uses its own store of food at first. Later, it uses light to make food.*

**1.** Roll up the blotting paper and put it in the jar. Place the bean between the paper and the jar. Wet the blotting paper. Keep the jar in a warm place.

**2.** After a few days, a root appears and grows downwards. It is searching for water, which the bean needs to grow.

**3.** A green shoot comes out of the bean and grows upwards. The shoot is looking for light, so it can grow. More roots grow down.

### Roots always grow down

Soak a bean in water for a day, then push a wire into it. (Ask an adult to help with this.) Fix the wire to the lid of the jar. Put some wet cotton wool in the jar, put in the bean and close the jar. Lay the jar on its side and leave it for a few days until a root begins to grow down. Then turn the jar so the root points upwards. Leave it, and the root changes direction so it grows down again.

*The shoot is growing downwards after the bean has been turned.*

# 51 Make a plant maze

Make a plant find its way through a maze! This shows how plants must have light in order to grow. They use the light to make food for themselves.

## You will need:

Two pieces of card | Jug of water | Scissors | Pot of compost | Runner bean seed | Long cardboard box

**1.** Cut a large window in one end of the box.

**2.** Cut a window in each card.

**3.** Plant the bean seed in the pot and water it.

*Soak the bean seed for a day before planting it.*

**4.** Fit a piece of card in the box. Put the pot in the bottom.

**5.** Put the lid on and stand the box in a warm, light place.

**6.** Insert the second piece of card when the plant grows and replace the lid.

**7.** Check the plant every few days. It bends in order to get through all the windows and reach the light.

*The young plant always grows towards a source of light.*

### Tall trees

Getting enough light can be a problem for the plants in a thick forest. Many trees grow very tall, competing with each other for light. Their leaves make the forest beneath them quite dark, but smaller types of trees and shrubs have adapted to this.

# 52 Grow a piece of plant

Plants do not grow only from seeds. You can cut up some plants, and new plants grow from the pieces! These are called "cuttings". Each one grows its own roots.

**You will need:**

Clear plastic bag    Rubber band    Secateurs    Pot of moist compost    Geranium plant

**1.** 👪 Ask an adult to cut a side shoot from the plant. It should have leaves, but no flowers.

**2.** Plant this cutting in the pot. Cover it with the plastic bag.

*Secure the bag with the rubber band.*

**3.** Over several weeks, your cutting will grow into a new geranium plant. You must keep the compost moist.

# 53 See a plant bubble

Plants need light to make their own food. You can show that plants also produce oxygen gas, which enters the air and water. Oxygen is important as nothing can live without it.

**You will need:**

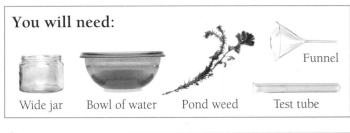

Wide jar    Bowl of water    Pond weed    Test tube    Funnel

**1.** Submerge the jar, pond weed, funnel, and tube in a deep bowl of water. Then, still underwater, arrange them as the picture shows. When you remove them from the water, the test tube remains full.

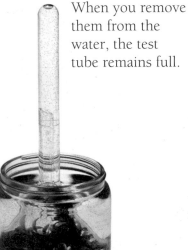

*Oxygen gas from the weed rises to the top of the tube.*

**2.** Place the jar in sunlight. The pond weed begins to bubble!

### Oxygen for life

It is important to have green water plants in an aquarium to release oxygen into the water. The fish breathe this oxygen. Green plants on dry land release oxygen into the air. The process in which plants use light to make food and oxygen is called "photosynthesis".

# 54 Test a plant for food

Plants make their own food in their leaves. This food is called "starch", and plants need it to grow. Test the leaves of a geranium plant to detect its food.

**You will need:**

Small dish
Iodine and dropper
Sticky tape
Scissors
Methylated spirit
Saucepan
Beaker
Black plastic
Tweezers

*No light can get through the plastic. The leaf uses up all its starch and makes no more.*

**1.** Tape plastic around some leaves. Leave the geranium in a light place for two days. Then pick a wrapped leaf and an unwrapped leaf.

**2.** Heat the water in the pan. Warm the spirit in the beaker. Dip both the leaves in the hot water, then leave them in the spirit.

*Putting the leaves in hot water and spirit removes the chlorophyll and makes them turn white.*

**3.** Now the leaves are almost white. Add iodine to them. The unwrapped leaf goes dark. The wrapped one does not.

*The substance that makes leaves green is called "chlorophyll". It helps the leaf make starch.*

*This is the wrapped leaf. It has no starch and so does not darken in iodine.*

*This green leaf has had no treatment. It still contains chlorophyll.*

*This is the unwrapped leaf. Treating it with iodine turns the starch in it a dark, blue-black colour.*

# 55 Grow your own mould

A fungus is a type of plant that does not produce seeds. Instead, it reproduces by releasing thousands of tiny specks called "spores" into the air. When the spores land, they grow into new fungi. Mould is an example of a fungus. You can grow some mould at home on bits of unwanted food.

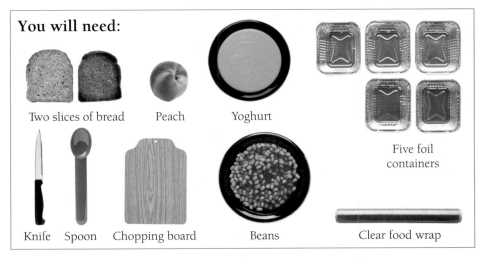

**You will need:**

Two slices of bread    Peach    Yoghurt    Five foil containers

Knife    Spoon    Chopping board    Beans    Clear food wrap

*You can use other fruit instead, but mould grows quicker on moist fruit such as oranges and peaches than it does on drier fruit such as bananas.*

**1.** 👫 Carefully cut the peach in half on a chopping board. Then place the two halves in a foil container.

*Make sure the toasted bread is very dry.*

**2.** 👫 Toast one slice of bread. Moisten the other slice with water. Cut the slices in half. Place the wet bread in the second foil container and the dry bread in the third.

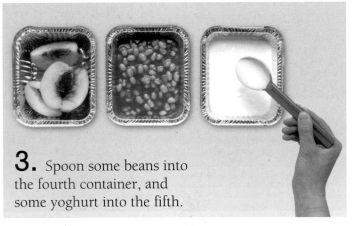

**3.** Spoon some beans into the fourth container, and some yoghurt into the fifth.

*Keep the dry and wet bread separate.*

Wet bread    Dry toast

*Make sure that the containers are tightly wrapped.*

**4.** Cover each container in clear food wrap. Leave the containers in a warm place for several days. Check on the containers every day, to see if anything has happened to the food.

Peach

Beans

Yogurt

### Make spore prints

Mushrooms are fungi. New mushrooms grow from the spores shed by fully grown mushrooms. You can make some spore prints to see how the spores drop from the mushrooms. Take two flat mushrooms with dark undersides. Remove the stalks and place the mushrooms on a sheet of white paper,with their undersides facing downward. Leave them for a day or two. When you lift the mushrooms, you will notice that they leave patterns of dark powder on the paper.

*The patterns are made up of the tiny dust-like spores that fall from the mushrooms.*

*Spore print*

**5.** Although you could not see them, tiny mould spores in the air landed on the different foods before you covered them up. After several days, mould will begin to appear on the food as the tiny mould spores grow. The mould grows faster on some foods than others. You may find that you get different coloured mould on different types of foods.

*Moisture and warmth help the spores to feed on the dampened bread, so the mould grows well.*

*Mould needs moisture to grow, so no mould appears on the dry, toasted bread.*

Wet bread

Dry toast

*Make sure you throw the mouldy food away. Do not touch it and wear kitchen gloves when you handle the containers.*

Peach

Beans

Yogurt

# SENSES

Your senses are your ability to see, hear, smell, and taste things, and to feel things when you touch them. Your senses make it possible for you to find out about the world around you, to do the things you want to do, and to survive. For example, your sight helps you to see what is happening and find your way about.

### Talking hands
One way to "talk" to someone who cannot hear is to use sign language. Deaf people watch the signs and use their sense of sight to understand what is being "said".

### On the ball
Games bring the senses of sight, hearing, and touch into action. Good players use all these senses well, reacting quickly to the sight and sound of the ball or to the other players, and throwing the ball accurately.

### Bombarding the senses
Our senses bring us exciting experiences – such as the bright lights and music at a concert.

### A tasty sight
We use our senses of sight and touch to help us choose good food, such as these vegetables. We then use our senses of taste and smell to enjoy eating them.

# 56 See how your ears work

When a sound enters your ears, it is changed into a signal. This travels to your brain, and you hear the sound. You can build a model ear to see how your ears do this.

**You will need:**

Cardboard tube    Torch    Clear food wrap

Piece of card    Rubber band    Modelling clay    Sticky tape    Sheet of paper

**1.** Stretch the plastic food wrap over the end of the tube. Secure it with the rubber band.

*The plastic must be smooth.*

**2.** Roll the sheet of paper to make a cone. Fasten it with sticky tape so that it does not unroll.

**3.** Push the small end of the cone into the open end of the cardboard tube. Tape it in place.

**4.** Stand the card on a table top. Lay the tube in front of it. Shine the torch on the plastic, so that a spot of light appears on the card.

*Fix the card with modelling clay.*

## Inside the ear

As sounds enter the ear, the eardrum vibrates. This in turn makes tiny bones vibrate and the vibration passes to the inner ear, which then sends signals to the brain, along the ear's nerve.

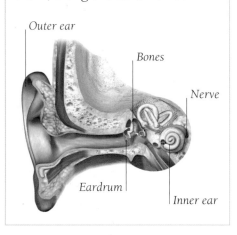

Outer ear

Bones

Nerve

Eardrum

Inner ear

*The light is reflected from the plastic. As the plastic vibrates, the spot of light shakes.*

*The plastic is like the eardrum at the end of your ear canal. Sounds make the eardrum vibrate, causing signals to go to your brain.*

*The outer ear (the cone) directs sound into the ear canal (the tube).*

**5.** Shout or sing loudly into the cone. The spot of light shakes very fast!

# 57 Find out how your eyes work

Build a model eye using a magnifying glass and a goldfish bowl, and find out how you see. Use the model to show how the eye forms an image of a human figure.

**You will need:**

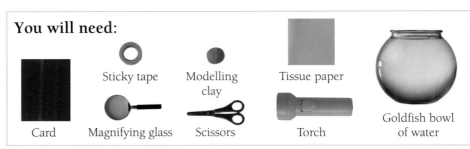

Sticky tape · Modelling clay · Tissue paper

Card · Magnifying glass · Scissors · Torch · Goldfish bowl of water

**1.** Tape the tissue paper to the side of the bowl.

**2.** Fix the magnifying glass in front of the bowl with modelling clay.

**3.** Fold the card and cut out half of a figure.

**4.** Fix the card in front of the magnifying glass.

### Entry to the eye

At the centre of each eye, there is a hole called the "pupil", where light enters the eye. The pupil changes size to control the amount of light entering the eye. If there is not much light, it gets larger and lets more in.

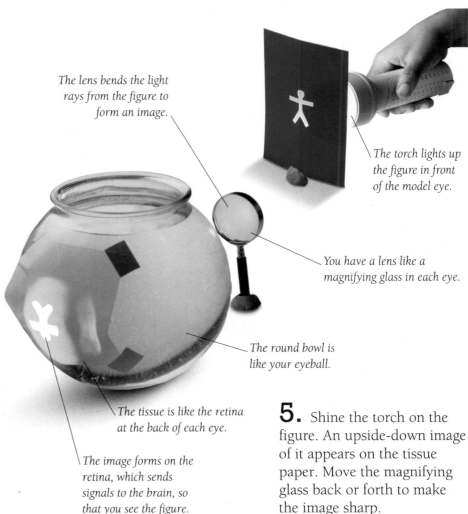

*The lens bends the light rays from the figure to form an image.*

*The torch lights up the figure in front of the model eye.*

*You have a lens like a magnifying glass in each eye.*

*The round bowl is like your eyeball.*

*The tissue is like the retina at the back of each eye.*

*The image forms on the retina, which sends signals to the brain, so that you see the figure.*

**5.** Shine the torch on the figure. An upside-down image of it appears on the tissue paper. Move the magnifying glass back or forth to make the image sharp.

# 58 See two pictures as one

Trick your eyes into seeing one picture when there are really two – one on each side of a piece of card. This experiment shows how you can see moving pictures on television and in the cinema.

**You will need:**

Two rubber bands

Scissors   Compasses

Colouring pens

White card

**1.** Make a circle on the card, using the compasses. Cut it out.

**2.** Draw a circle on the card. Make two holes, one on each side.

**3.** Turn the card over and draw a cross on the other side.

**4.** Thread a rubber band through each of the holes in the card.

**5.** Twist the bands by holding them and turning the card.

*Your eyes hold an image of an object for a short time after the object disappears.*

*The card whirls so fast that images of the circle and cross overlap in your eyes.*

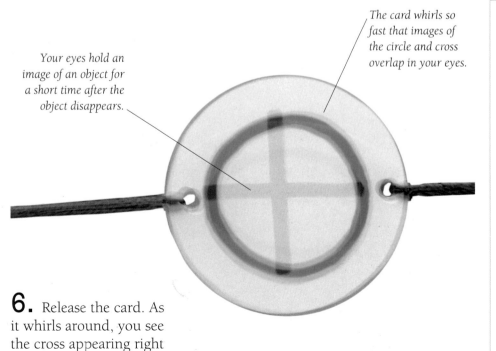

**6.** Release the card. As it whirls around, you see the cross appearing right inside the circle.

**Moving pictures**
Films are made up of long strips of still pictures, each one slightly different from the one before. The pictures appear rapidly on the screen, one after the other. When you watch a film, your eyes do not see each picture separately. They overlap and appear to move.

# 59 Build a wobble detector

Having two eyes helps you judge distances well. With a wobble detector, you can find out just how useful it is to have two eyes. Close one eye and you'll find you can't help wobbling!

**You will need:**

Two jar lids    Bare stiff wire    Scissors    Three pieces of covered wire with bare ends

Bulb-holder and bulb    Modelling clay    Sticky tape    Battery    Screwdriver

*Bend the stiff wire into several curves.*

**1.** Use modelling clay to fix the ends of the stiff wire to the jar lids.

**2.** Using one piece of covered wire, connect one end of the stiff wire to the battery.

**3.** Connect the second piece of covered wire to the battery and the bulb-holder.

**4.** Take the last piece of covered wire and fix one end to the bulb-holder. Make a loop with the other end.

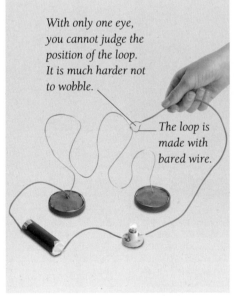

*With only one eye, you cannot judge the position of the loop. It is much harder not to wobble.*

*The loop is made with bared wire.*

**5.** Place the loop around the stiff wire. Try to move the loop along the wire without touching it. Try it with both eyes open, then with one eye closed. Which is easier?

**Looking forward to a meal**
An owl has two large eyes that face forwards. These help the owl to judge the position of the prey it is hunting. Like the owl, you use two eyes to see how near or how far away objects are. Your brain combines the images from both eyes to do this.

# 60 Change your ears around

Sounds come to you from all sides. Having two ears makes it possible to work out where sounds are coming from. Trick your hearing so sounds come from the wrong directions.

**You will need:**

Two plastic funnels

Sticky tape

Insulating tape

Two lengths of plastic tubing

Fabric

Length of wood

*Fix fabric over the end of each tube.*

*A sound from one side goes to the ear on the other side.*

**1.** 👫 Fix each tube to a funnel. Tape the tubes to the wood, as the picture shows. Fit the tubes into your ears so they fit closely. Do not force them in.

**2.** Ask a friend to walk by, making a noise. The sounds seem to move the opposite way to your friend!

**Steering by sound**
A bat uses its sense of hearing to find its way around in the dark. As it flies, it makes high sounds that are almost impossible for our ears to hear. These sounds bounce off nearby objects and return to the bat's ears. The bat uses these returning sounds to locate objects around it – and to find the insects it hunts for food.

# 61 Take a taste test

If you test your sense of taste, you will find that it is not just your mouth that enables you to tell one flavour from another – your sense of smell is very important, too.

**You will need:**

Three small glasses

Three different types of pure fruit juice

Large glass of water

Scarf

**1.** Ask a friend to blindfold you with the scarf. Taste each juice in turn. You will find it easy to recognize the flavours.

*Wash your mouth out between tastings.*

**2.** Hold your nose and taste the juices again. Now it is more difficult to identify the juices!

*The juices now have similar flavours.*

# 62 Test your sense of touch

You can feel something as soon as it touches your skin, but you may not be able to detect its shape or size. Make a touch tester to find out just how much you can feel.

**You will need:**

Pins    Colouring pens    Cloth

Thick card    Compasses    Scissors    Ruler

**1.** Use the ruler and compasses to draw three circles on the card, one inside the other.

*The circles should be 3, 6, and 9 cm (1.2, 2.4, and 3.6 in) across.*

**2.** Cut out the large circle and colour in the three zones.

*The three circles form the three zones of your touch tester.*

Middle zone

Central zone

Outer zone

**3.** Ask a friend to blindfold you with a cloth.

**4.** Your friend should stick some pins in the central zone.

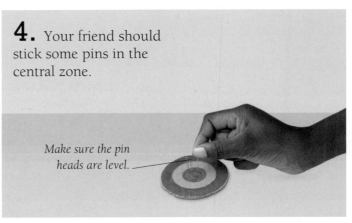

*Make sure the pin heads are level.*

*Do not let the card touch the skin.*

*Your fingertips are very sensitive. You can feel each one of the pins in the central zone.*

*Your palm is less sensitive. You can feel each pin in the middle zone, but not in the central zone.*

*Your arm is not very sensitive. You can only tell how many pins there are in the outer zone.*

**5.** Ask your friend to press the pin heads gently against your arm. How many pins can you feel? Try again with the pins stuck in the middle and outer zones. Then test your palm and fingers.

# 63 Check your reaction time

You need all your senses to tell you when you suddenly have to take action. Sometimes you need to move very fast. Do this test to find out just how quick off the mark you really are.

**You will need:**

Colouring pens

Pencil

White paper

Scissors

Glue

30-cm (12-in) ruler

**1.** Draw around the ruler on the paper. Cut out the strip and mark six equal bands.

**2.** Colour the bands and then glue the strip to the ruler.

**3.** Ask a friend to hold the ruler so that one end is between your thumb and your forefinger.

*Keep your thumb and forefinger about 1 cm (0.4 in) apart.*

**4.** Suddenly, your friend releases the ruler. Try to catch it! The colour you grab tells you your reaction time – the time between sensing something and beginning to move.

Slow reaction time

Medium reaction time

Fast reaction time

**Wait for it!**
As soon as a kitten sees something move, it darts into action and begins to chase it, just like an adult cat after its prey. Animals often have very fast reactions. They need these when they are hunting for food, or escaping from enemies.

# SOUND AND MUSIC

Sounds are all around us. There are beautiful sounds in nature – such as birds singing and water lapping. There are frightening sounds, too, like thunder. We use sounds when we speak to each other, and music brings us great pleasure. A siren makes a sound that warns us of danger. There are so many different sounds – but none of them is anything more than a shaking movement in the air.

**Sound signals**
We often use sounds as signals. Blowing a whistle in a game can mean "stop" or "go".

**Sound pictures**
This is a picture of an unborn baby – inside its mother! The picture was made using special sounds called "ultrasound".

**The speed of sound**
You hear the bang a balloon makes as soon as it bursts. This is because sound travels quickly from the balloon to your ears. It moves at 340 m per second (1,115 ft per second) – slightly faster than most airliners.

**Songs of the sea**
Many animals make sounds to communicate with each other. Whales "sing", and their songs travel far under water.

**Making music**
Music is fun, whether you listen to it, play it, or sing. You can make good music with home-made instruments like this drum. Experiment 69 on page 80 explains how to make a drum.

# 64 See some sound

When anything makes a sound, it "vibrates" or shakes rapidly. This makes the air around it vibrate, too. Air vibrations called "sound waves" spread out through the air. When they reach your ears, you hear a sound. Show how sounds make the air shake.

**You will need:**

Rubber band  Plastic bowl  Big saucepan  Piece of plastic

Uncooked rice  Scissors  Large spoon  Sticky tape

**1.** Cut a piece of plastic slightly bigger than the bowl.

**2.** Stretch the plastic over the bowl, using the rubber band.

*Stretch the plastic as tightly as you can.*

**3.** Tape the edges of the plastic firmly to the bowl.

**4.** Sprinkle a few grains of the rice on the stretched plastic.

*As you hit it, the pan vibrates and gives out sound waves.*

*Sound waves travel through the air and make the plastic vibrate.*

**5.** Hold the saucepan near the plastic. Hit it with a spoon. The rice jumps up and down!

### Getting the vibrations
This picture shows a boy listening to a tuning fork. The tuning fork is giving out sound waves. If you could see the air vibrations in sound waves, they would look like the blue curves. Thousands of these vibrations reach your ears every second as you hear a sound.

*The grains of rice jump up and down as the plastic vibrates. You can see this clearly from the side.*

# 65 Make a sound gun

Sound waves batter your ears – though you may not feel them. Loud sounds can make things move. Prove this by firing a sound wave at a target and making it shake.

**You will need:**

Scissors     Thin strip of paper     Rubber band

Thin plastic     Cardboard tube     Stiff paper     Sharp pencil     Sticky tape

**1.** Draw around the tube to make a circle on the paper.

**2.** Cut out the circle from the paper.

**3.** Use the sharp end of the pencil to make a small hole in the centre of the circle.

**4.** Tape the circle to one end of the tube.

**5.** Using the rubber band, fix the plastic over the other end.

**6.** Fold the paper strip and tape it to the top of the table.

### Sliding snow

Sound can cause an "avalanche" – when ice and snow crash down the side of a mountain. Sound waves from a loud noise disturb the snow and start it moving.

*Tapping the plastic causes a sound wave to travel down the tube.*

*The sound wave makes the air move and shake the strip.*

**7.** Point the end of the tube with the hole at the paper strip. Tap the plastic and the strip shakes.

*The hole directs the sound wave towards the strip.*

# 66 Make a coat-hanger clanger

Sound waves travel through other materials as well as through air – sometimes more effectively. This simple experiment uses cotton thread to carry sounds to your ears.

**You will need:**

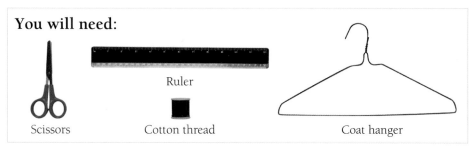

Scissors     Ruler     Cotton thread     Coat hanger

*When you have tied the threads, slide them to opposite corners of the hanger.*

**1.** Measure out and cut two pieces of thread about 30 cm (12 in) long. Tie one end of each thread to the base of the coat hanger.

*As the coat hanger bangs against the chair, it makes a gentle ringing sound.*

**2.** Wind one thread around the first finger of each hand. Lift the hanger up by the threads and then swing it against a chair. Listen to the noise it makes.

### Sounds in your head

Strike a tuning fork on a table. Gently press the base against your head. The sound is louder than when you first heard it! Like the thread in the above experiment, the bones of your skull carry sounds to your ears much better than the air.

*Sound travels more easily up the thread to your ears than it does through the air.*

**3.** Put the fingers wrapped in cotton thread in your ears, but do not press them in too hard. Swing the hanger against the chair again. Now the hanger sounds like the clanging of a huge bell!

# 67 Bounce a sound

Sometimes, you hear sounds that have not come straight to you. Show how sounds may reach your ears after they have first bounced off another object.

**You will need:**

Ticking watch

Two cardboard tubes     Plate     Cork mat     Several books

**1.** Build two piles of books, both the same height.

**2.** Lay one tube on each of the piles of books.

**3.** Hold the watch close to one ear and check that it ticks.

**4.** Place the watch in the end of one of the tubes.

*Sound waves travel down the tube to the plate.*

**5.** Listen at the end of the other tube. You cannot hear the watch tick – until a friend holds the plate near the ends of the tubes.

*The sound waves bounce off the hard plate and travel up the tube to your ears.*

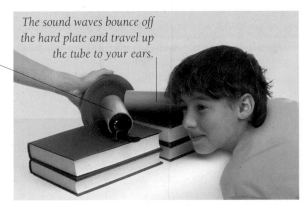

### Good sounds

In a concert hall, sound waves from the stage bounce off the walls. This helps improve the quality of the sound the audience hears.

*Sound waves bounce off walls.*

**6.** Get your friend to hold a cork mat instead of the plate. Now you cannot hear the watch any more.

*The soft cork soaks up the sound waves.*

# 68 Make a paper banger

Make a loud bang with nothing more than a sheet of paper! The banger produces a quick and large movement of air, forming a sudden and powerful sound wave. This rushes through the air towards you and you hear it as a bang.

**You will need:**

Sheet of stiff paper measuring about 30 cm by 40 cm (12 in by 16 in)

*Fold here*

**1.** Fold the longer edges of the paper together. Then open it out.

*First fold*

**2.** Fold the corners into the first fold.

*First fold*

**3.** Fold the paper in half along the first fold. Then fold it in half again, lengthways.

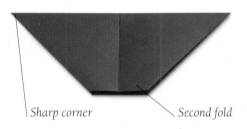

*Sharp corner*    *Second fold*

**4.** Open out the second fold.

**5.** Fold down the two sharp corners.

**6.** Fold the paper back along the second fold to make a triangle shape.

## Thunder and lightning

A flash of lightning heats the air so that it expands very suddenly. This sends a powerful sound wave through the air. We hear this as a clap of thunder.

*A flap of paper springs out and makes the air move suddenly. You hear this as a bang.*

**7.** 👫 Grip the banger firmly by the two sharp corners. Flick it down quickly – and it makes a loud bang!

# 69 Beat some drums

Make a tin drum and a tom-tom. They make different kinds of sounds, but they work in the same way. When you hit a drum's stretched skin, it vibrates. This makes the air inside the drum vibrate – and out comes the sound.

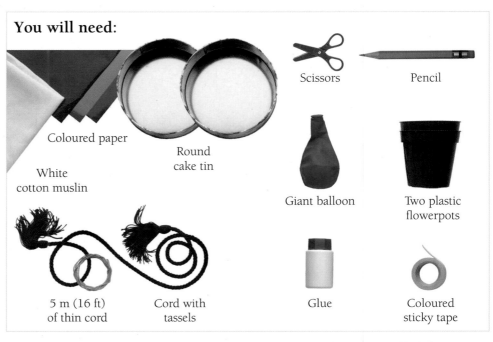

**You will need:**

Coloured paper

White cotton muslin

Round cake tin

5 m (16 ft) of thin cord

Cord with tassels

Scissors

Pencil

Giant balloon

Two plastic flowerpots

Glue

Coloured sticky tape

**1.** Decorate the tin with coloured paper. Tape the thick cord firmly to opposite sides of the tin.

**2.** Cut off the balloon's neck. Stretch the balloon over the tin and tape it. The tin drum is ready.

**3.** Using the pot, draw two circles on the muslin. Then draw two larger circles around each one.

**4.** Cover the pots with coloured paper. Then tape the bottoms of the pots firmly together.

**5.** Cut out the large circles of muslin. Cut flaps in each edge, as far as the second circle.

Make sure the holes are evenly spaced.

**6.** Fold in and glue the flaps of both circles. With the pencil, make 16 holes around each edge.

**7.** Thread thin cord through the holes. Place a circle over each pot. Pull the cord tight and tie it.

**8.** Loop the rest of the cord through the cords in the edges of the circles. Pull it tight and tie it.

**9.** Spread glue over each circle. Tighten the cord again. When the glue is dry, the tom-tom is ready.

*The tape holds the balloon skin, so it stays stretched.*

*Tightening the cord stretches the muslin skin more and gives a higher note.*

*Squares of coloured paper and strips of tape.*

*Do not strike the drum skins too hard, as they may burst or break.*

**10.** Put the cord of the tin drum around your neck. Beat the drum with a stick, such as a pencil. Hold the tom-tom under your arm or between your knees. Beat it with your fingers.

**Drum kit**
This is the standard drum kit played by a drummer in a band. It has several drums of different sizes, and the drummer plays them all – including a large drum played with a foot pedal. It also has several cymbals.

# 70 Strike up a tune

Make your own xylophone. This instrument has wooden bars that vibrate, producing musical notes when you strike them. Your xylophone is made with pencils.

**You will need:**

Pencil sharpener · Thick coloured card · Poster paint · Scissors · Paintbrush · Felt · 8 fat pencils · Rubber solution glue · Beads · Wooden skewers · Ruler

**1.** Use the shapes below to make a cardboard frame. Paint and glue felt along the ridges.

**2.** Use the sharpener to shorten the pencils as shown. Rest them on the frame.

**3.** Play the pencil xylophone with beaters made from wooden skewers and beads.

*Make the sides of the frame this shape, 21 cm (8.5 in) long.*

*Make the long end of the frame this shape, 15 cm (6 in) long.*

These shapes are smaller than the ones you need. Make yours the sizes shown.

*Make the short end of the frame this shape, 11 cm (4.5 in) long.*

# 71 Play a pipe

You can make music from a set of pipes. All you have to do is blow across the open ends. This makes the air inside each pipe vibrate, producing a musical note. Different lengths of pipe give different notes.

**You will need:**

Card · Glue · Scissors · Coloured sticky tapes · About 1.5 m of (5 ft) plastic pipe · Coloured ribbon · Modelling clay

**1.** Cut the pipe into pieces, each 1 cm (0.5 in) longer than the last. Decorate them with tape.

**2.** Tape the pipes together to make a set. Glue the ribbon to a strip of card, and glue it over the tape.

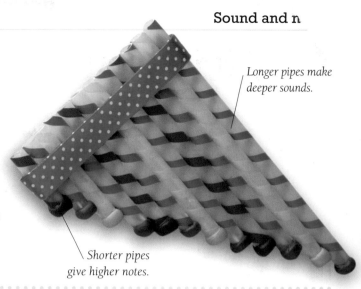

*Longer pipes make deeper sounds.*

**3.** Roll the modelling clay into small balls. Push one ball of modelling clay into the bottom of each pipe.

**4.** Hold the set of pipes against your bottom lip. Move the pipes to and fro, and blow into different pipes to play a tune.

*Shorter pipes give higher notes.*

## 72 Blow a horn

You can make a horn from a hosepipe and funnel! Close your lips firmly together and put them to the end of the horn. Blow air through your lips and the horn will sound. This happens because your lips make the air inside the horn vibrate.

**You will need:**

Cord with tassels

75 cm (30 in) of hosepipe

Funnel

Scissors

Pencil

Coloured sticky tape

**1.** Decorate the funnel with tape. Push it into one end of the hose and fix it with tape.

**2.** Tape around the other end to make the mouthpiece. Loop the hose and fix the pencil to it.

**3.** Decorate the horn with strips of tape and with the cord. Now your horn is ready to blow.

*Blow through the mouthpiece*

**4.** The horn produces only a few notes. You can get these by pressing your lips tighter together as you blow, or letting them relax a little.

# Build a banjo

A banjo has four strings, stretched tightly. You play the banjo by plucking the strings with your fingers. The strings vibrate very fast, producing musical notes. You can strum a rhythm by plucking all the strings together. Or you can play one note after another, to pick out a tune. You can make each string play several notes.

**You will need:**

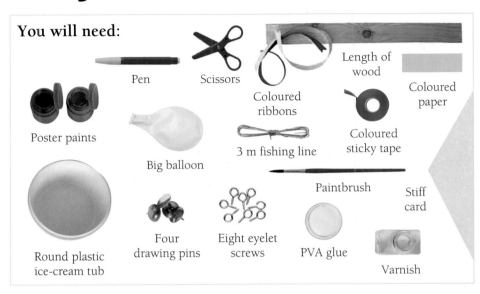

Pen
Scissors
Coloured ribbons
Length of wood
Coloured paper
Poster paints
Big balloon
3 m fishing line
Coloured sticky tape
Round plastic ice-cream tub
Four drawing pins
Eight eyelet screws
Paintbrush
PVA glue
Varnish
Stiff card

**1.** Cut two "I" shapes under the rim of the tub, opposite each other. Make them as wide as the end of the wood.

**2.** Bend the flaps of the "I" shapes outwards. Push the end of the wood through the holes. Pin the flaps to the wood.

**3.** Paint and varnish the wood and the tub. Mix glue with the paint you use for the tub. Paint lines across the wood.

**4.** Cut off the neck of the balloon. Stretch the balloon over the tub and tape it to the sides. Paint a design on it.

**5.** Partly screw four eyelet screws into each end of the wood. Make sure you can turn each screw in either direction.

**6.** Make two triangular bridges of card and paper. Make one the same width as the wood and the other three times as wide.

**7.** Make four strings by cutting the fishing line. Tie these strings securely to the two sets of eyelet screws.

**8.** Insert the two bridges under the strings, as the picture shows. Turn the eyelet screws to tighten the strings.

**9.** Decorate the banjo by fixing pieces of ribbon of different colours to the eyelet screws. Your banjo is now ready to play.

*Hold a string down to change its note. The notes get higher as you move your hand towards the tub. The lines show you where to press the strings.*

*Tightening the string makes it sound higher. Slightly loosening the string lowers its note.*

*Make each bridge by folding and glueing pieces of card and paper. Cut four notches in one edge to hold the strings.*

*The bridges raise the strings so they are free to vibrate.*

**10.** Tune the banjo by tightening the strings, so each one gives a different note.

**Busy fingers**
The guitar is like a banjo, except that it has six strings. When you press a guitar or banjo string, you change the length of the part of the string that vibrates. This changes the note made by the string when you pluck it.

# MAGNETS

Magnets have mysterious powers. They can pull things towards them, and push other magnets away. This power drives the electric motors that are inside many machines we use – such as hairdryers and trains. Magnets make it possible for television sets, radios, and music players to produce sounds. Computers use magnets to store information.

### Magnetic mineral
The first magnets were pieces of black mineral called "lodestone". Lodestone attracts objects such as this paperclip.

### Lights in the sky
The Earth is a huge magnet. Its magnetism makes these coloured lights appear in the sky near the north and south poles.

### North, south, east, west
You use a compass to find directions. It makes use of the Earth's magnetism, which causes the needle always to point north.

### Pick and stick
A magnet can pick up objects made of iron or steel. The objects stick to the ends of the magnets.

### Gadgets and magnets
Many gadgets around you, including computers, music players, and earphones contain magnets. The hard drives computers use to store information also use magnets.

### Flying home
Pigeons can usually find their way home. Some scientists believe they use the Earth's magnetism to sense direction, rather like a compass.

# 74 Charm a snake, fly a kite

Make a snake rear up and raise a kite into the sky – all with the amazing power of magnets. At the same time, you can find out which kinds of things magnets attract.

**You will need:**

Selection of magnets

Small objects, paperclips, and a pencil

Scissors

Cotton thread

Ruler

Sticky tape

Glue

Coloured felt

**1.** Copy the snake pattern onto felt. Cut out the snake and decorate it with coloured felt.

**2.** Tie a short length of thread to a paperclip. Fix the paperclip to the snake's head.

**3.** Tape a magnet to the end of the ruler. Tape the loose end of the thread firmly to the table.

Snake pattern

**4.** Hold a magnet close to the objects. See how it picks up only the ones made of iron and steel.

*The magnet attracts the paperclip. Raise the magnet so that the paperclip pulls the thread tight.*

**5.** Move the ruler and magnet around, above the snake. The snake rises and dances, like a snake-charmer's snake. If the snake does not rise, use a stronger magnet or a shorter thread. Try making other shapes in the same way – like this brightly coloured felt kite.

# 75 Compare the strength of magnets

Some magnets are stronger than others. This experiment shows you how to test a magnet's strength and compare the strengths of different combinations of magnets.

**You will need:**

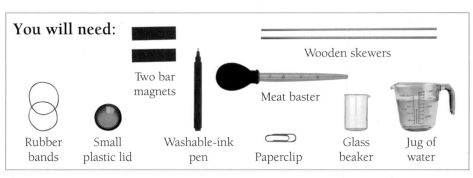

Two bar magnets

Wooden skewers

Meat baster

Rubber bands

Small plastic lid

Washable-ink pen

Paperclip

Glass beaker

Jug of water

**1.** Place an upright bar magnet between two wooden skewers, midway along their lengths. Loop rubber bands over the skewers to hold the magnet tightly in place.

**2.** Add water to the glass beaker until it is about one-third full. Put the paperclip in the plastic lid. Gently place the lid on the water's surface, so that it floats.

**3.** Rest the wooden skewers holding the magnet on the rim of the beaker. Make sure that the bottom end of the magnet is positioned over the plastic lid.

**4.** Using the baster, carefully add drops of water to the beaker. Stop adding water when the paperclip jumps up and clings to the magnet.

**5.** Mark the water level on the outside of the beaker. Repeat the experiment using two magnets. Make sure the magnets' repelling ends are alongside each other.

**6.** This time, the water level is much lower. Two magnets are stronger than one, so less water has to be added before they pull the paperclip towards them.

**Moving magnets**

A maglev (short for magnetic levitation) train uses strong magnets and electricity to move. A magnetic coil running along the track repels magnets on the underside of the train, which makes the train hover (levitate). Electricity flows through the coils, which creates magnetic pushes and pulls that move the train forward.

# 76 Build a magnetic car

You can use two ordinary magnets to make a model car move. It works because two magnets can either attract or repel each other when they are brought close together. The way in which they move depends on which ends of the magnets are facing each other.

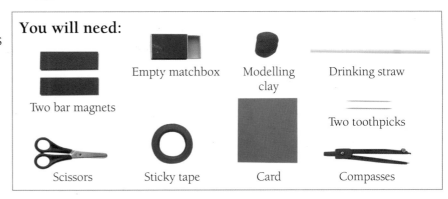

**You will need:**

Two bar magnets

Empty matchbox

Modelling clay

Drinking straw

Two toothpicks

Scissors

Sticky tape

Card

Compasses

**1.** Firmly tape one of the magnets to the inside of the matchbox tray.

**2.** 👤 Cut the straw in two pieces. Make each piece the same size as the matchbox.

**3.** Tape the pieces of straw to the outside part of the matchbox. Slide in the tray.

**4.** 👤 Using the compasses, draw four circles on the card. Carefully cut them out.

**5.** 👤 Push the toothpicks through the straws. Fix the card circles to them.

*Put modelling clay over the sharp points.*

*The magnet in the car is attracted or repelled by the magnet in your hand.*

**6.** Place the matchbox car on a table top. Bring the other magnet close. The car rolls towards or away from the magnet.

*Turn the magnet around, and the car rolls in the other direction.*

# 77 Detect a magnet's field

Around every magnet, there is a "magnetic field" where the magnet can exert its powers to push or pull. Normally, a magnetic field is invisible – but there is a way you can see it.

**You will need:**

Two clear glass or plastic containers

Golden syrup

Pencil

String

Two bar and two horseshoe magnets

Iron filings

Clear food wrap

**1.** Pour a tablespoon of iron filings into a jar of syrup. Stir it well, mixing the filings evenly. Then pour some mixture into two clear glass or plastic containers.

**2.** Place two bar magnets under one container. Place two horseshoe magnets at opposite sides of the other.

**3.** Fill the third container with the mixture. Wrap a bar magnet in clear food wrap. Tie it with string to a pencil and then hang it in the container.

## What do you see?

The filings form a pattern within the magnets' magnetic fields. The pattern shows you the direction of the pull from the magnets on the iron filings.

The two bar magnets are pushing each other away. The pattern of the filings shows how the two magnetic fields are working in opposite directions, keeping the magnets apart.

The two horseshoe magnets at opposite ends of a container both attract iron filings. The filings show how the magnetic fields loop round from one end of each magnet to the other end.

A magnetic field extends in all directions around a magnet. You can see this clearly with the magnet hanging in the syrup. It looks the same whichever way you turn it.

*Throw the syrup away after the experiment – do not try to eat it!*

*Covering the magnet stops it getting sticky.*

**Magnetic attraction**
A magnet can pick up a whole chain of small, steel objects. The magnet's field turns each one of the objects into a small magnet, which goes on to attract another steel object.

## 78 Separate a mixture

It is usually very difficult to separate two powders that have been mixed together. But you can do it easily if one of the powders is magnetic and the other is not.

**You will need:**

Plate of iron filings     Magnet     Plate of sand

**1.** Tip the plate of iron filings so that they drop into the sand. Stir them together with your fingers.

**2.** Keep stirring until the sand and the iron filings are completely mixed up.

**3.** Bring a magnet close to the plate. It will pick up the iron filings and leave the sand behind.

# 79 Construct a compass

The Earth is a huge magnet with its own magnetic field. This field is strong enough to make another magnet turn if it is free to move. A magnet will always turn to point north.

**You will need:**

Needle | Jug of water | Toothpick | Sticky tape

Polystyrene tile | Bar magnet | Modelling clay | Compasses | Plastic pot

*The disc must fit inside the pot.*

**1.** Use the compasses to draw a disc on the tile. Carefully cut it out and colour it.

**2.** Stick a blob of modelling clay in the middle of the pot. Push the toothpick upright in it.

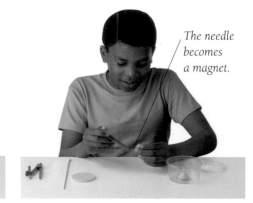

*The needle becomes a magnet.*

**3.** Draw one end of the magnet along the needle, about 30 times, in the same direction.

**4.** Tape the needle to the disc. Rest the disc on the stick. Fill the pot with water.

*North pole of the Earth's magnetic field*

**5.** When water reaches the disc, it floats and turns. One end of the needle points north, as a compass needle does. Mark this end.

*South pole*

*When the needle is magnetised, one end gains a north pole. The north pole of the Earth's magnetic field attracts the north pole of the needle.*

**Getting directions**

The needle of a compass is a light magnet balancing on a pivot. As you turn the compass around, the red end of the needle always swings to point north. If you turn the compass until "N" for north is below the needle, it will show all directions correctly.

# 80 Make an electromagnet

You can make a strong magnet by using electricity. It is not like an ordinary magnet, which is always magnetic. You can switch the power of an electromagnet on and off.

**You will need:**

Long screwdriver

Sticky tape

Wirestrippers

Scissors

Switch (see experiment 87)

4.5 V battery

Lots of paperclips

2 m (6.5 ft) coated wire

**1.** 👫 Cut a long piece of wire. Strip the ends and tape part of it to the handle of the screwdriver.

**2.** Coil most of the rest of the wire around the screwdriver. Tape the last turn.

**3.** Connect the wire, and another short piece of wire, to the battery and switch, as the picture shows.

*The paperclips contain steel wire that is attracted to the electromagnet.*

*Electromagnet with 60 turns*

*Connect the short wire to the other terminal.*

*Electromagnet with 40 turns*

*Electromagnet with 20 turns*

**4.** The screwdriver is now an electromagnet. Press the switch, and the screwdriver picks up some paperclips! Open the switch, and the paperclips fall off.

**Metal mover**
This crane has a powerful electromagnet to lift bits of scrap iron and steel. The scrap sticks to the electromagnet when it is switched on, and can be moved by the crane. When the current is switched off, the scrap falls away.

*The coil of wire produces a magnetic field when electricity flows through it. More turns of wire give a stronger field.*

# 81 Build a buzzer

A buzzer uses magnetism to make a loud buzzing sound. It contains an electromagnet, like the one on page 93. The buzzer's button is a kind of switch. When you press it, electricity can travel to the electromagnet in the buzzer. The electromagnet causes movements within the buzzer. These movements make the noise.

**You will need:**

Steel nail file

Switch (see experiment 87)

Scissors

Thick cardboard

Rubber band

3 m (9.8 ft) covered wire

Sticky tape

Wirestrippers

4.5 V battery

Metal drinks can

Iron or steel bolt

Modelling clay

Cotton reel

**1.** Strip both ends of the wire. Wrap it firmly around the bolt 200 times. Fix the bolt to the cardboard with modelling clay.

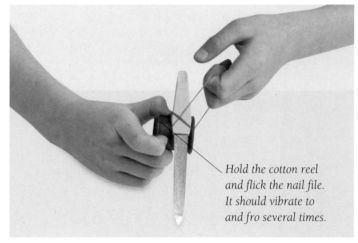

*Hold the cotton reel and flick the nail file. It should vibrate to and fro several times.*

**2.** Using the rubber band, attach the handle of the nail file firmly to the cotton reel.

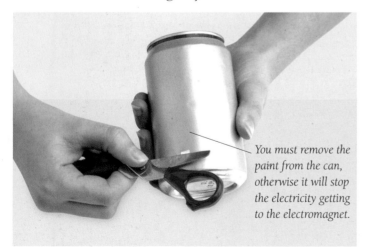

*You must remove the paint from the can, otherwise it will stop the electricity getting to the electromagnet.*

**3.** With the scissors, scrape away some paint at the base of the can. Do this again on the opposite side of the can.

**4.** Tape one end of the wire to the metal part of the nail file. Fix the cotton reel to the cardboard, as shown in the next picture.

*Fix the wire to the scraped part of the can.*

**5.** 👪 Cut two wires and strip the ends. Fix one wire to the battery and the can and the other to the battery and the switch.

**6.** Stick the can to the card, with the end of the nail file touching the other scraped part. Connect the switch, as the picture shows.

*Every time the nail file strikes the can, electricity flows through it to the electromagnet. This becomes magnetic, and pulls the file away from the can. Opening this gap stops the electricity, and the electromagnet stops working. The nail file springs back and strikes the can again.*

*You may need to move the bolt nearer to the nail file to make the buzzer work.*

*The bolt and wire form an electromagnet.*

*Electricity flows from the battery, through the can, and into the nail file. Then it passes through the electromagnet and switch, back to the battery.*

**7.** Press the switch, and a loud buzz comes from the can! The nail file vibrates rapidly to and fro and strikes the can again and again. When you release the switch, the nail file stops – and so does the buzzing.

**Magnetic machine**
Modern telephones work rather like a buzzer does. Inside the earpiece there is a small electromagnet. When electricity flows through the electromagnet, it causes a strip of metal to vibrate. This vibration produces the sound of the caller's voice.

# ELECTRICITY

Electricity makes all kinds of machines work. It can have great power – it drives the fastest trains in the world, for example. But electricity can also power very small machines, such as MP3 players and calculators. Most machines you use at home, such as television sets and vacuum cleaners, use "current electricity". This is the kind of electricity that comes from batteries and power points in your home. There is another kind of electricity, called "static electricity", which you can make yourself.

**Power from water**
The electricity we use in our homes is made in power stations. This one is a "hydroelectric" power station. It uses the energy of moving water, coming through a dam.

**Plug into power**
You plug electrical machines like this hairdryer into power points. Electricity travels from power stations along wires and into the power points.

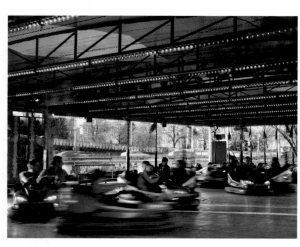

**Electric ride**
These fairground cars pick up current electricity from overhead wires. In each car, the electricity powers an electric motor that turns the wheels.

**Electrical attraction**
If you rub a balloon on a T-shirt or a jumper, it gets static electricity on its surface. This causes it to stick to things – walls, ceilings, even you!

# 82 Bend some water

When you rub some objects, they gain electricity. This electricity stays in the objects, so it is called "static", which means it is something that stays in the same place. Static electricity has amazing power to attract things – even running water!

**You will need:**

Balloon          Balloon pump

**1.** Pump up the balloon. Stretch the neck and tie a knot in it, so the air does not escape.

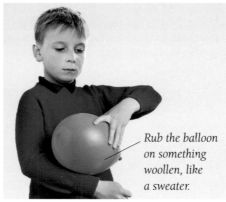

*Rub the balloon on something woollen, like a sweater.*

**2.** To give static electricity to the balloon, rub it .

**3.** Hold the balloon near running water from a tap. The water bends towards the balloon!

# 83 Make a propeller

Static electricity can repel objects, as well as attract them. If you rub two pens, they will repel each other, because they have both gained static electricity.

**You will need:**

Cotton thread          Two plastic pens          Silk scarf

**3.** Static electricity pushes the pen round like a propeller!

**1.** Tie some thread around the middle of one of the pens. Position the thread so that the pen balances when it is dangled in the air.

**2.** Rub one end of each pen with a silk scarf. Dangle one pen from the thread and bring the two rubbed ends towards each other.

# 84 Jump with electricity

Get some paper people jumping up and down. You can do this using the static electricity you get when you rub a balloon. Because static electricity can repel objects as well as attract them, the paper people jump both ways.

**You will need:**

Pen

Scissors     Balloon     Balloon pump     Thin paper

**1.** Draw some small people on the paper.

**2.** 👫 Carefully cut them out. Make as many people as you like.

**3.** Place all your paper people on a tabletop.

**4.** Pump up the balloon until it is quite big. Then tie a knot in its neck so no air escapes.

**5.** Rub the balloon on some woollen clothes.

## Electric fields

Run a comb through your hair a few times and then see how it picks up bits of paper. An invisible electric field forms around an object as it gains static electricity. The comb's electric field reaches the bits of paper and attracts them so that they cling to it. A comb can also make your hair stand up, for the same reason.

*At first, the electricity in the balloon attracts the paper people.*

*After the people have stuck to the balloon, the static electricity repels them.*

*The people jump up and down again and again as they are attracted and repelled.*

**6.** Hold the balloon about 10 cm (4 in) above the people. They jump up and down!

# 85 Wave a magic wand

Use the power of electricity to make yourself into a magician. At the wave of a wand, you can make some little silver balls dance on a record! In fact, it is static electricity, not magic, that makes them dance for you.

**You will need:**

Sharp pencil

Glass or plastic bowl

Silver balls for cake decoration

LP record

Clean, dry handkerchief

**1.** Rub the record briskly with the handkerchief. It gains static electricity.

*Use an old record that no one wants to play any more.*

**2.** Straight away, put the record on top of the bowl. Have the silver balls ready.

### Safe from lightning
A tall building often has a lightning conductor. This is a pointed rod that reaches from the top of the building to the ground. It can weaken the static electricity in the clouds, and this can stop lightning striking the building. If it does strike, the conductor leads it safely to the ground.

*Conductor*

**3.** Drop a few silver balls on the record. They roll about, and then suddenly stop.

*Some parts of the record have more static electricity and attract the balls.*

*The balls roll away to other parts of the record with more static electricity.*

**4.** Bring the pencil towards the record. As the point gets near each ball, it leaps away and dances about!

*The electricity gets weaker where the pencil points.*

# 86 Build a charge detector

Rubbing an object such as a plastic comb or a balloon gives it a charge of electricity. Find out how to detect an electric charge – then see how the charge can move.

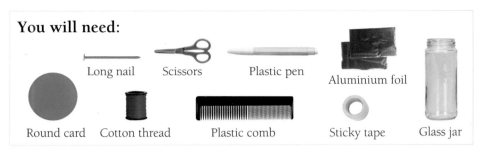

**You will need:**

Long nail  Scissors  Plastic pen  Aluminium foil

Round card  Cotton thread  Plastic comb  Sticky tape  Glass jar

**1.** Ask an adult to push the nail about two-thirds of the way into the centre of the card.

**2.** Tie the middle of a piece of thread tightly near the sharp end of the nail.

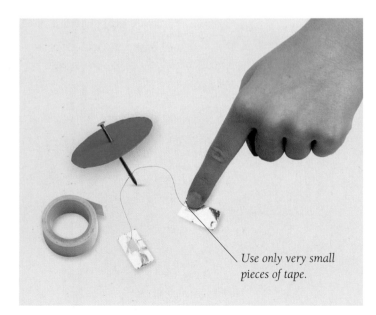

*Use only very small pieces of tape.*

**3.** Cut two strips of foil and tape them to the ends of the thread.

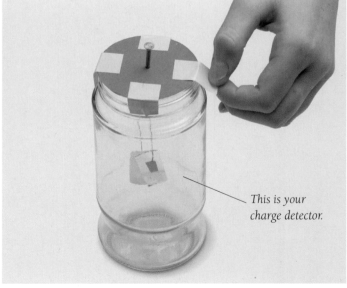

*This is your charge detector.*

**4.** Place the card on the jar, with the foil strips hanging inside. Tape it in place.

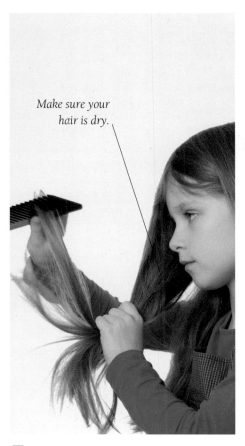

*Make sure your hair is dry.*

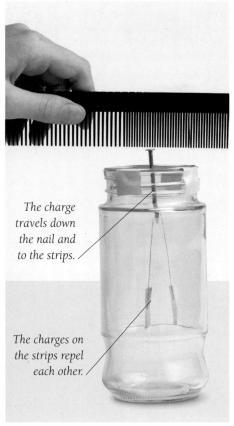

*The charge travels down the nail and to the strips.*

*The charges on the strips repel each other.*

*The charge travels out of the strips and to your hand.*

**5.** Run the comb through your hair several times, quite quickly.

**6.** Run the comb along the head of the nail. The foil strips move apart. This shows the comb has an electric charge, which passes to the strips.

**7.** Touch the top of the nail. The strips collapse and hang down.

*The electric charge cannot flow out through the plastic pen, so the strips keep their charge.*

**8.** Charge the detector again. Now touch the nail with a plastic pen. The foil strips do not collapse.

**Hair raiser**
When you pull off a jumper you may see sparks. These are caused by static electric charges that leap between the jumper and your head.

# 87 Construct a circuit

Current electricity moves. When a battery is connected up properly, current electricity comes from one of its terminals. It then follows a path called a "circuit" back to the other one.

**You will need:**

Coated wire

Bulb

Battery (same voltage as bulb)

Two paper fasteners

Wirestrippers

Screwdriver

Scissors

Thick cardboard

Bulb-holder

Steel paperclip

**1.** 👥 Cut two pieces of wire. Carefully strip away the plastic ends and then twist the bare strands of wire together.

**2.** Firmly fix one end of each wire to each terminal of the battery. Make sure the bare wire is touching the terminal.

**3.** Make one wire touch the base of the bulb and the other one touch the side. This forms a circuit and the bulb lights up.

**4.** Screw the bulb into the bulb-holder. Fix the wires to the bulb-holder as the picture shows. The bulb lights up again.

**5.** Break the circuit by removing one of the wires from the battery. The bulb goes out because electricity cannot pass the gap.

**6.** 👥 Cut a third piece of wire. Strip the ends and twist the strands of wire, in the same way as you did in step 1.

**7.** Fix one end of the third piece of wire to the battery terminal that is no longer connected.

**8.** 🕴 Cut out a piece of card measuring 3 cm by 5 cm (1.2 in by 2 in). This is the base of a switch.

**9.** Wind the end of the wire from the bulb-holder around a paper fastener. Push it through the card.

*Closing the switch completes a circuit. Electricity flows from one battery terminal, through the wires to the switch and bulb, and back to the other terminal.*

**10.** Repeat step 9 with the wire from the battery. This time, put a paperclip round the paper fastener.

*Current electricity flows into and out of the wires fixed to the terminals.*

**11.** Close the switch by touching the paperclip to the first paper fastener. The bulb lights up.

### Printed circuits

Machines such as television sets and computers contain many electrical parts. Instead of travelling through wires, current electricity flows along lines printed on boards inside the machine. It goes to working parts of the machine mounted on these boards.

# 88 Probe for electricity

Electricity does not flow through all materials. Wires that carry electricity are often coated with plastic to stop electricity passing from the wire into other materials that it touches. Make a bug that shows if electricity can pass through something.

**You will need:**

Wirestrippers  Coated wire  Sticky tape

Two 1.5 V batteries  3.5 V bulb  Three pipe cleaners  Coloured card and paper  Aluminium foil

Sequins  Scissors  Bulb-holder  Glue  Screwdriver

**1.** Tape the top of one battery firmly to the base of the other, with a foil square between them.

*Strip the ends of the wires.*

**2.** Cut lengths of wire 25, 12, and 8 cm (10, 5, 3 in) long. Tape the 25-cm (10-in) wire to one battery.

*Screw the bulb into the holder.*

*12-cm (5-in) wire*

*8-cm (3-in) wire*

**3.** Connect the 12-cm (5-in) and 8-cm (3-in) wires to the holder. Tape the 8-cm (3-in) wire to the other battery.

**4.** Tape the bulb-holder to the batteries. Fix paper around the batteries and wires to make a bug.

*Make big eyes with ovals of card and sequins.*

*25-cm (10-in) wire attached to base of batteries*

*Make legs with pipe cleaners.*

*12-cm (5-in) wire attached to bulb-holder*

*Aluminium foil "conducts" or passes electricity. It completes a circuit so that the bulb lights.*

*Tightly wrap the ends of the wires in balls of foil.*

**5.** Touch the foil balls on the bug's feelers to different kinds of materials. The bulb lights up if electricity can pass through the material.

# 89 Build a battery

A battery contains chemicals which it uses to make electricity. You can make your own simple battery with salt, foil, and coins. These contain the chemicals needed to produce electricity.

**You will need:**

Two wires with stripped ends     Six copper coins     Sticky tape     Pen     Saucer

Paper towels     Scissors     Aluminium foil     Warm, salty water     Earphones

**1.** Draw and cut out six coin-sized foil circles and six paper ones.

**2.** Tape one wire to a coin, and the other wire to a foil circle.

**3.** Dip a paper circle in the warm salty water.

**4.** Put the foil circle with the wire in the saucer. Place the wet paper circle and a coin on top.

**5.** Build up more layers of foil, wet paper and coins. The coin with the wire goes on top. This is your battery.

**6.** Fix the end of one wire to the base of the plug of the earphones.

**7.** Put on the earphones. Scrape the end of the other wire on the tip of the plug. You hear crackles in the earphones!

*When you place aluminium, salt, and copper together, they make electricity.*

*The electricity goes to the earphones and makes the sounds.*

**Inside a battery**
These are the materials that go inside a long-life battery. Electricity comes from the terminals at the top and bottom of the battery.

*Top of battery*

*Case of battery*

*Layers of chemicals react together when a circuit is connected to the battery. Electricity flows through the circuit. After a time, all the chemicals are used up and the battery no longer works.*

**DO NOT EVER try to take a battery apart. It can be DANGEROUS.**

*Base of battery*

# 90 Make a merry-go-round

Electric motors power many modern machines. You can even buy a small one to work a merry-go-round. Electricity makes the shaft of the motor spin and drive the merry-go-round.

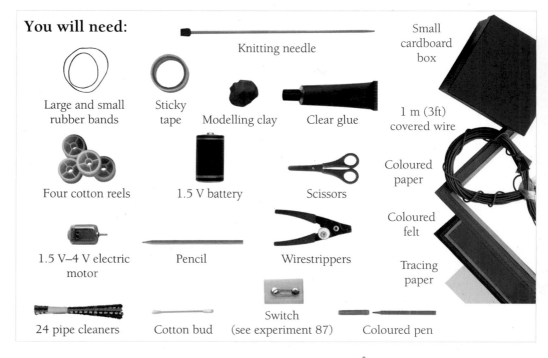

**You will need:**

Knitting needle

Large and small rubber bands

Sticky tape

Modelling clay

Clear glue

Small cardboard box

1 m (3ft) covered wire

Four cotton reels

1.5 V battery

Scissors

Coloured paper

Coloured felt

1.5 V–4 V electric motor

Pencil

Wirestrippers

Tracing paper

24 pipe cleaners

Cotton bud

Switch (see experiment 87)

Coloured pen

Eagle pattern

Swallow pattern

**1.** Cut three pieces of wire and strip the ends. Cut a piece of cotton bud and place it on the shaft of the motor.

**2.** Connect the three wires to the motor, battery, and switch as the picture shows. Glue the motor to the side of the box.

**3.** Roll a strip of paper around the knitting needle. Remove the strip and push it firmly into the centre of one of the cotton reels.

**4.** Glue the reel to the bottom of the box. Stick the other three reels to the knitting needle with modelling clay, as the picture shows.

**5.** Stretch the large rubber band around the box. Fit the small rubber band around the bottom reel on the needle.

**6.** Make frames for six birds to sit on the merry-go-round. Use pipe cleaners to form the head, body, and wings of each bird.

**7.** Trace the eagle and swallow patterns on felt. Cut out six bird shapes and tape them to the pipe cleaner frames.

**8.** Using pipe cleaners and tape, fix the six birds to the top two reels. Fit the knitting needle into the reel in the box.

**9.** Stretch the small rubber band so that it fits over the piece of cotton bud on the shaft of the electric motor.

Blue swallow

Yellow, pink, and blue eagle

Adjust the big rubber band so that it holds the knitting needle upright.

Pipe cleaner supports

Pink and blue eagle

**10.** Press the switch, and the birds spin around! Electricity from the battery turns the shaft of the motor. This moves the rubber band, which turns the knitting needle.

The small rubber band must fit tightly and not slip on the shaft and reel.

# MOTION AND MACHINES

The world around you is on the move. People and animals walk, run, swim, and fly. The wind blows, rivers flow. Machines are on the move, too, performing tasks for people. A machine, like everything that moves, works because a force pushes or pulls it. The force can come from a powerful engine or motor – or just human muscles.

**Good opening**
Automatic doors work themselves. They send out invisible rays. These detect movement so the doors open as people approach.

**Quick thinking**
A calculator is a machine that does sums for you. It works at lightning speed.

**Perfect performer**
A robot is a very advanced kind of machine. It can be instructed to carry out complicated tasks, and it does them perfectly.

**Getting going**
These two girls are exerting a force on each other. They push each other, and this makes them both move backwards.

**Handy machine**
A corkscrew is a machine. It removes a cork from a bottle – something hard to do with your bare hands.

# 91 Build a wheelbarrow

Machines can give you more strength! Build your own wheelbarrow and move a heavy load of stones. The wheelbarrow is a "lever" – a machine that can increase the force you use to move things.

## You will need:

Plastic bag — Short pencil — Stones — Two equal lengths of wood — Cotton reel — Sticky tape — Card — Shoe box — Scissors

**1.** Put the stones in the bag and lift them. You need to exert a lot of force.

**2.** 👫 Cut the card to the same size as the box. Tape the card inside to make two sections.

**3.** Tape the lengths of wood firmly to the bottom of the box.

**4.** Stick the pencil through the cotton reel. Tape it to the ends of the lengths of wood.

*It is easier to lift the stones now they are in the barrow.*

*The lengths of wood form a lever that tilts around the wheel.*

**5.** Put the bag of stones in the back of the barrow. Try lifting it.

*You need less effort when the load is nearer the wheel.*

*When you use a lever, your hands move farther than the distance the load moves. This extra movement gives the lever the extra force to lift the load.*

*The reel is the wheel of the barrow. It must turn easily.*

**6.** Move the bag of stones to the front of the barrow. Now it is very easy to lift the heavy load.

# 92 Get a jet going

Airliners fly around the world at high speed. They have large jet engines that produce a powerful jet of air to drive the airliner through the sky. Show how a jet engine works by flying a balloon at speed across a room.

## You will need:

Length of thread

Balloon pump

Sticky tape

Balloon

Drinking straw

**1.** Feed the thread through the straw. It must move easily.

*Make sure the thread is tight.*

**2.** Stretch the thread across a room. Stick two pieces of tape to the straw.

*No air must escape from the balloon.*

**3.** Blow up the balloon. Hold the neck, and attach the balloon to the straw.

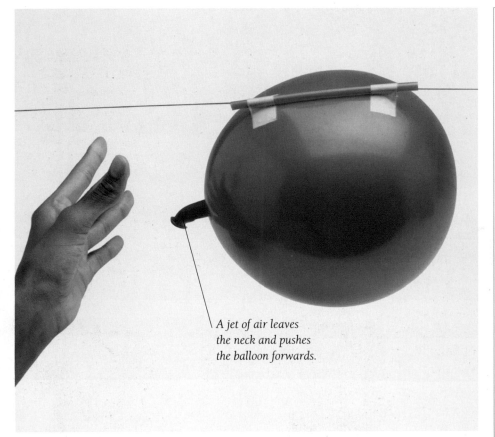

*A jet of air leaves the neck and pushes the balloon forwards.*

### Fast movers
Jet engines power the fastest cars in the world as well as high-speed aircraft. A jet engine sucks in air at the front and heats this air with burning fuel. It then sends the hot air blasting out from the back of the engine. This forces the aircraft or car forwards at very high speed.

**4.** Let go of the balloon. It rushes along the thread at high speed!

# 93 Build a turbine

A turbine is an engine powered by a moving liquid or a gas. You can build your own turbine out of straws, and power it with the air from your lungs!

**You will need:**

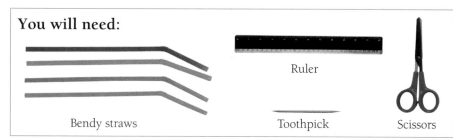

Bendy straws

Ruler

Toothpick

Scissors

**1.** 👥 Cut the long ends off two bendy straws, about 4 cm (1.5 in) from the bend. Push the end of one straw into the end of the other.

*Straws rest on toothpick.*

*Bend the end so that it points horizontally.*

*The air you blow through the straw turns the "turbine"!*

**2.** Place a toothpick in the short end of a third straw. Slot the two connected straws over the toothpick. Hold the device horizontally and blow through the long straw.

# 94 Test for friction

It's much easier to slide on something smooth, like ice, than on a rough surface. This is because rough surfaces create more friction than smooth ones, and friction slows things down.

**You will need:**

Screwdriver

Drawing pins

Wooden block

Two lengths of wood

Hinge and screws

Pen

Protractor

Ruler

Quarter circle of card

Test surfaces such as felt, sandpaper, and card

**1.** 👥 Screw the hinge to the two lengths of wood. Now one length can lie flat while the other slopes.

**2.** Using the protractor and ruler, draw a scale of angles on the card. Fix this to the bottom length of wood with the drawing pins. Place a test surface on the top length of wood.

**3.** Place the block on the end of the surface. Tilt the surface until the block starts to slide.

*You can use oil or water to reduce friction.*

*The angle is the amount of friction the surface creates*

# 95 Move in a circle

A special kind of force is needed to make something move in a circle. It is called "centripetal" force. See how this force keeps an object moving in a circle instead of flying off.

**You will need:**

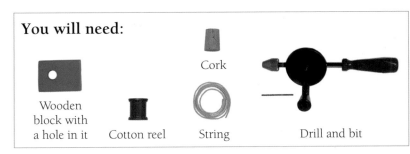

Cork

Wooden block with a hole in it

Cotton reel

String

Drill and bit

*The cork tries to fly outwards.*

*The weight of the block holds the cork back. This weight is the centripetal force.*

**1.** Drill a hole through the centre of the cork. Tie a big knot in one end of the string and thread the other end through the cork and the cotton reel.

**2.** Tie the other end of the string to the block. Check that the string runs easily through the cotton reel and that the knot stops the cork from coming off the string.

**3.** Hold the cotton reel. Move it so that the cork whirls round. The block rises as the cork circles around the reel.

# 96 Engage a gear

Gears are pairs of wheels which link so that one turns another. Gears of different sizes turn at different speeds, and make it possible for machines to change speed. Try making some gears of your own.

**You will need:**

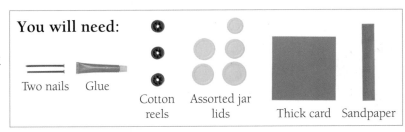

Two nails   Glue

Cotton reels

Assorted jar lids

Thick card   Sandpaper

**1.** Glue sandpaper strips around the edges of the lids. Glue on the reels as the picture shows.

**2.** Push nails through the card. These are axles for your gear wheels.

**3.** Place a different-sized wheel on each nail, so that they touch. Turn them, using a reel as a handle.

# 97 Make an automatic machine

Machines often need people to operate them in order to work properly. But some need no one to control them. This automatic machine sorts big marbles from small ones, all on its own!

**You will need:**

Straw
Kebab stick
Long cardboard box
Two short cardboard boxes
Large and small pieces of card
Scissors
Glue
Sticky tape
Modelling clay
Big and small marbles

**1.** Cut openings in the long box and in one of the short boxes. The picture shows where these should be. Glue the short box to the top of the long box.

*Two openings*

*Two openings*

**2.** Fold the small piece of card lengthways to make a chute. Use pieces of modelling clay to fix it to the top of the other small box.

*Small piece of modelling clay*

**3.** Make channels in the large piece of card by folding the sides. Tape a straw underneath and insert the stick.

*Folds*

**4.** Stick two small marbles to one of the channels with modelling clay. Place the stick on two blocks of modelling clay, so the weighted side touches the table.

**5.** Line up the boxes, the chute, and the card, as the picture shows. Roll a small marble down the chute.

*The small marble rolls into the upper box.*

*Big marbles are heavy enough to tilt the card, but small marbles are not.*

*Small marbles*

**6.** Roll a big marble down the chute. The card drops, and the marble goes into the lower box.

## Mail machine

Letters and parcels go through automatic sorting machines. These can detect postcodes marked on the mail, and sort letters and parcels going to different towns into different compartments.

# 98 Construct a fan

Keep cool – with a hand-powered fan. This machine uses a belt that works in the same way as a gear. It makes the fan spin faster than the handle that you turn to make it work. Many machines have parts like these that work together at different speeds.

**You will need:**

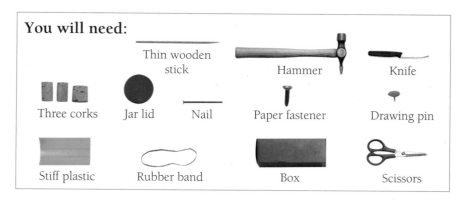

Thin wooden stick

Hammer

Knife

Three corks

Jar lid

Nail

Paper fastener

Drawing pin

Stiff plastic

Rubber band

Box

Scissors

*Put the holes 5 cm (2 in) from the top and bottom of the box.*

*Make one hole in the middle of the lid and the other near the edge.*

**1.** 🕴 Ask an adult to make two holes in the front of the box, and another in the back, opposite one of the first holes. Ask the adult to then make two holes in the jar lid, using the nail.

**2.** 🕴 Using the drawing pin, fix a cork to the jar lid. This is the handle of your fan.

*Push the fastener through the lid and the second hole in the box. The handle should turn easily.*

**3.** Attach the handle to the box with the paper fastener.

*Slant the slits.*

**4.** 🕴 Ask an adult to cut four evenly spaced slits in another cork. Now two corks are in use.

**5.** Cut four long strips from the plastic. Make them as wide as the slits in the cork.

**6.** Push the plastic strips into the slits, and push one end of the stick into the cork.

*Push the stick right through the box.*

*The rubber band should fit without much stretching.*

*The rubber band is a belt that links two wheels – the lid and the cork.*

**7.** Push the stick through the other two holes in the box. The stick should poke out from the back of the box.

**8.** Push the third cork onto the end of the stick. Loop the rubber band around this cork and the handle. Your fan is now ready.

**Riding at speed**

The chain on a bicycle is a belt that causes the back wheel to turn faster than the pedals. When you change gear, the chain moves from one of the gear wheels on the hub to another. The size of the gear wheels affects the speed at which the back wheel turns. Bigger wheels make the bicycle go faster.

*The blades spin faster than the handle turns.*

**9.** Turn the handle of the fan. The blades spin rapidly and blow air forwards!

*The jar lid is a bigger wheel than the cork. This causes the cork to turn faster than the lid.*

# 99 Build a water wheel

Many machines have a motor or an engine to produce the force they need to make them move. The first kind of motor or engine was the water wheel. It uses the power of flowing or falling water to drive a machine. Water wheels are still used today.

**You will need:**

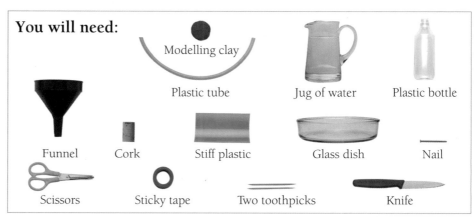

Modelling clay

Plastic tube          Jug of water          Plastic bottle

Funnel          Cork          Stiff plastic          Glass dish          Nail

Scissors          Sticky tape          Two toothpicks          Knife

**1.** Use the knife to cut four slits in the side of the cork. Space them out evenly.

**2.** Cut out four pieces of stiff plastic. Make them all the same length as the cork.

**3.** Fit the pieces of plastic into the slits. This is the water wheel.

*Make sure the blades fit tightly.*

**4.** Using the nail, pierce two holes in opposite sides of the bottle.

**5.** Cut off the bottom of the bottle, making sure the edge is straight so the bottle can stand upright.

**6.** Push a toothpick into one end of the cork. Then fit it into one hole in the bottle.

**7.** Push the other toothpick through the other hole and into the cork.

*The water wheel must spin easily.*

*Put modelling clay on the points of the toothpicks.*

**8.** Push the funnel into one end of the piece of plastic tube. Wind sticky tape around the funnel and tube to hold them firmly together.

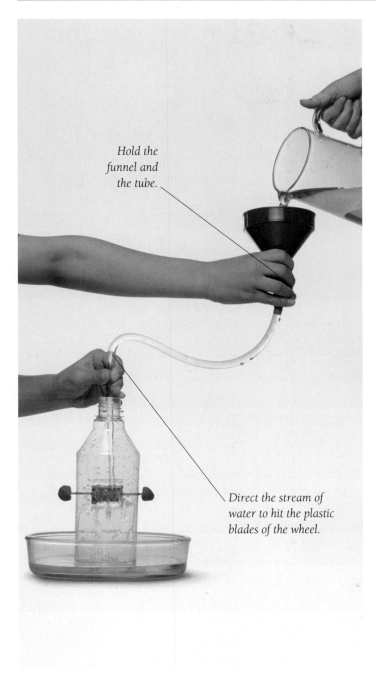

*Hold the funnel and the tube.*

*Direct the stream of water to hit the plastic blades of the wheel.*

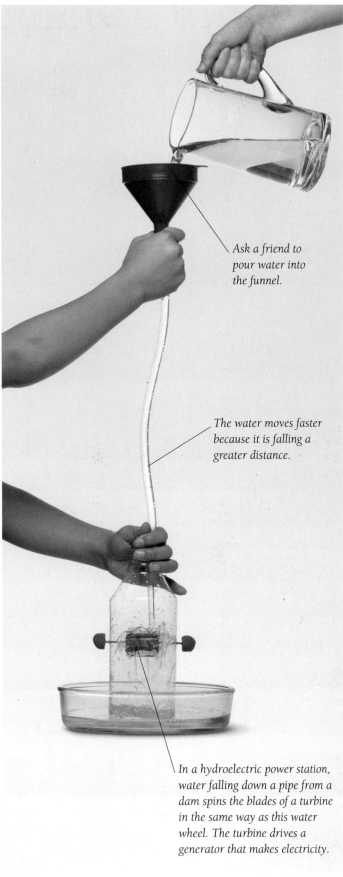

*Ask a friend to pour water into the funnel.*

*The water moves faster because it is falling a greater distance.*

**9.** Place the bottle in the dish. Fit the tube into the neck of the bottle. Pour water into the funnel, and the water wheel spins round.

*In a hydroelectric power station, water falling down a pipe from a dam spins the blades of a turbine in the same way as this water wheel. The turbine drives a generator that makes electricity.*

### Air power

These are wind turbines. They work in the same way as water wheels, but use moving air instead of water. The wind spins the blades, which drive a generator in each turbine to make electricity.

**10.** Raise the funnel. The water flows faster as it hits the blades of the water wheel, making it spin more quickly.

# 100 Lift a load with water

Raise a heavy weight – with just a little water! Using water in this way is called "hydraulics". Very powerful machines that lift, push, or press things work by hydraulics. It greatly increases the force that they produce.

**You will need:**

Rubber band · Plastic tube · Sticky tape · Heavy book · Plastic bottle

Water · Balloon · Scissors · Funnel · Can

**1.** Fit the neck of the balloon over the end of the tube. Seal it tightly with sticky tape.

**2.** 🏃 Cut the top off the bottle. Make a hole in the side, near the base of the bottle.

**3.** Push the balloon through the hole in the side of the bottle.

**4.** Tape the funnel firmly to the other end of the tube, as the picture shows.

**5.** Place the can inside the bottle on top of the balloon. Then lay the heavy book on the bottle.

**6.** Lift the funnel and pour some water into it. The balloon slowly swells – and lifts the heavy book!

**Big digger**
Powerful excavators like the one in this picture use hydraulics. Pipes carry a liquid from a pump to cylinders, where the liquid pushes out pistons with great force. The pistons drive the bucket into the ground and raise a heavy load of soil.

*Raise the funnel above the book.*

*The swelling balloon exerts enough pressure to push the heavy book upwards.*

*The weight of the water in the tube pushes water into the balloon.*

# 101 Build a crane

A crane is able to lift a heavy load high in the air. It has a wheel called a "pulley" to produce a lifting force, while a "counterweight" stops the crane tipping over as it lifts a heavy weight.

**You will need:**

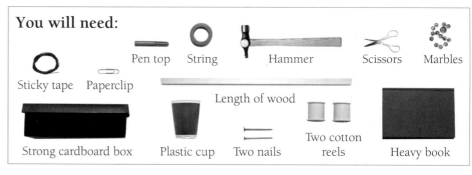

Sticky tape  Paperclip  Pen top  String  Hammer  Scissors  Marbles

Strong cardboard box  Length of wood  Plastic cup  Two nails  Two cotton reels  Heavy book

*Make sure the reels can turn easily.*

**1.** Nail one reel to the end of the wood and nail the other reel near the other end.

**2.** Cut a hole in the box. Insert the wood so that it sticks out at an angle.

*The wood must fit tightly and not move.*

**3.** Cut a short piece of string. Tape it to the cup to make a handle.

**4.** Push the pen top into the lower reel. Tape one end of the rest of the string to this reel.

*The pen top is your handle.*

**5.** Loop the string over the upper reel. Hold the end firmly and wind the string onto the lower reel.

*The book is a counterweight. Its weight prevents the weight of the load from pulling the crane over.*

*The upper reel is a pulley wheel. It changes the downward force of the handle into an upward force that lifts the load.*

**6.** Bend the paperclip to make a hook. Tie it to the end of the piece of string.

**7.** Place the book on the box. Fill the cup with marbles and hook it to the crane. Wind the handle to lift the load of marbles.

# INDEX

## Acknowledgements

Dorling Kindersley would like to thank:
Andrea Needham, Nicola Webb, and Tracey White for design assistance. Andy Crawford, Jane Burton, Michael Dunning, Pete Gardner, Frank Greenaway, Colin Keates, Dave King, Ray Moller, Stephen Oliver, Gary Ombler, Tim Ridley, Clive Streeter, and Kim Taylor for the commissioned photography. Models Kirsty Burns and Paul Cannings.

## Picture credits

The publisher would like to thank the following for their kind permission to reproduce their photographs:
(Key: a-above; b-below/bottom; c-centre; f-far; l-left; r-right; t-top)

6 Dreamstime.com: Natalia Lisovskaya (tl). 7 Alamy Images: D. Hurst (tc). 9 Dreamstime.com: Georgerudy (cra); Tomas Pavlasek (c); Kurt (cr); Smellme (bc). 14 Dreamstime.com: Odua (tr). 16 Dreamstime.com: Monkey Business Images (tl). Fotolia: dundanim (cl). 17 Science Photo Library: David Hay Jones (bc). 18 Dreamstime.com: Alvarracrazy (tr); Igor Zakharevich (tc). 19 Fotolia: Andrzej Tokarski (cb). 23 Corbis: Ralph White (tc). 26 Dorling Kindersley: Rough Guides (br). 27 Dreamstime.com: Mr.smith Chetanachan (bl). 30 Dreamstime.com: Pavel Losevsky (bl); Veniamin Kraskov (tl); Peter Wilson (tr); Photoeuphoria (br). 33 Corbis: Tetra Images (bl). 35 Dreamstime.com: Catonphoto (bc). 36 Corbis: Larry Williams (bc). Dorling Kindersley: The Natural History Museum, London (tr). Dreamstime.com: Exopixel (tc). 37 Dreamstime.com: Robert Paul Van Beets (bc). 38 Dreamstime.com: Jacek Chabraszewski (bl); Marcomayer (tr). 39 Dreamstime.com: Scottbeard (crb). 41 Getty Images: AFP / Yasuyoshi Chiba (br). 45 Dreamstime.com: Martiapunts (bl). 46 Dreamstime.com: Dmitrijs Gerciks (bl). 47 Science Photo Library:

PHILLIP HAYSON (br). 48 Alamy Images: PhotoSpin, Inc (c). Dorling Kindersley: Rough Guides (tr). Dreamstime.com: Tyler Olson (tl). 50 Dorling Kindersley: Rough Guides (br). 51 Getty Images: Photographer's Choice / Jeff Smith (bc). 54 Dreamstime.com: Aliaksandr Mazurkevich (crb/Washing soda); Geografika (c); Mitgirl (cb); Lawrence Wee (crb/Ammonia). 57 Dreamstime.com: Alterfalter (bc). 58 Corbis: Wavebreak Media Ltd. (tr). 59 Dreamstime.com: Dusan Kostic (br). 61 Dreamstime.com: Valentyn75 (br). 66 Corbis: Brian Mitchell (tl); Carolina Faruolo (tr); Rubberball / Erik Isakson (cl, cr); Mika (cb). 67 Dorling Kindersley: Medimation (bl). 68 Dreamstime.com: Pavel Losevsky (bl). 69 Getty Images: AFP / Martin Bureau (br). 70 Dreamstime.com: Honourableandbold (crb). 74 Corbis: amanaimages / Doable (bc). Dreamstime.com: Beflydream (cr); Cristianzamfir (tl); Darren Brode (tr); Sergey Dolgikh (cl). Getty Images: age fotostock / Masa Ushioda (clb). 76 Dreamstime.com: Boris Panasyuk (bl). 77 Alamy Images: Caro / Robert Seeberg (bl). 82 Dreamstime.com: Feng Yu (cra). 85 Getty Images: Photodisc / Andy Sotiriou (br). 86 Alamy Images: Chad Ehlers (tr). Dreamstime.com: Creativefire (clb). 88 Dreamstime.com: Yinan Zhang (br). 93 Dreamstime.com: Dan Van Den Broeke (bc). 95 Dreamstime.com: Romangorielov (br). 96 Corbis: Blend Images / Jose Luis Pelaez Inc (br); Thanh-Khoa Tran (tr). Dreamstime.com: Kobby Dagan (tl); Satori13 (cl). 99 Dreamstime.com: Milosluz (tc). 100 Dreamstime.com: Daniel Korzeniewski (tc/Thread); Katrina Brown (tc/Handmade Paper); Valerii Stoika (tc/Comb). 101 Dreamstime.com: Coramueller (tl). 103 Dreamstime.com: Christian Bridgwater (br). 105 Dreamstime.com: Sarah2 (bl). 108 Dreamstime.com: Antikainen (cr). iStockphoto.com: flashgun (tr). 110 Dreamstime.com: Tom2898 (br). 113 Getty Images: Bloomberg via Getty Images (bc). 118 Dreamstime.com: Nael_pictures (bl)

Jacket images: Front: Dreamstime.com: Keko64 tc/ (Bulb)

All other images © Dorling Kindersley
For further information see: www.dkimages.com